Art of Negotiation

Contents

Chapter 1 - Understanding Basic Principles   **10**

  A definition   **11**

  Negotiation and consultation   **14**

  Is negotiation necessary?   **16**

  Stages in negotiation   **17**

    Preparation   17

    During negotiation   19

    Implementation   19

  Key points   **20**

Chapter 2 - Weighing Relative Strengths   **21**

  Decision-making power   **23**

  The power of influence   **24**

  The strength of the case   **25**

  Determination   **27**

  Key points   **28**

Chapter 3 - Setting the Objectives   **30**

  Deciding the top line   **32**

  The bottom line   **34**

  Credibility   **35**

  Winning and losing   **36**

  Key points   **37**

Chapter 4 - Assessing the Other Side's Case   **38**

  Discovering the other party's aims   **39**

  The other side's facts and arguments   **41**

A hidden agenda   42

Key points   43

Chapter 5 - Setting the Style and Scene   44

The style or tone   45

Who to involve   47

Pace and timing   49

Location   50

Seating and refreshments   51

Documentation   53

Key points   55

Chapter 6 - Setting the Agenda   56

The formal agenda   57

Influencing the agenda   59

Key points   60

Chapter 7 - Probing the Other Side's Case   62

Exposing flaws   62

Errors of fact   63

Omissions of fact   63

Misuse of statistics   64

Faulty logic   64

Appeals to emotion   65

Testing credibility   66

Key points   67

Chapter 8 - Strengthening One's Own Case   68

Sanctions   68

Tactics   70

The introduction of new issues   70

Attaching conditions to concessions   73

The use of emotion 74

    Key points 75

Chapter 9 - Timing and Adjournments 77

    The duration of sessions 79

    Adjournments 80

    Key points 82

Chapter 10 - Searching for Common Ground 83

    Listening 84

    The use of humour 86

    Reading between the lines 87

    Looking for links 88

    Key points 91

Chapter 11 - Working Towards Agreement 92

    Periodic summaries 92

    Hypothetical suggestions 93

    Helping the other party to move 95

    Saving face 97

    Constructive compromise 99

    Key points 100

Chapter 12 - Clinching Agreement 101

    Closing the deal 101

    Ensuring all points have been included 103

    Ensuring full understanding 104

    Avoiding 'fudge' 105

    Key points 107

Chapter 13 - Securing Implementation 108

    An agreed implementation programme 108

Joint implementation   **110**

Information and explanation   **111**

Key points   **112**

Chapter 14 - Handling Breakdown   **113**

Unilateral action   **114**

Third party intervention   **115**

• Conciliation or mediation   115

• Arbitration or court rulings   116

Key points   **119**

Chapter 15 - Negotiating by Letter and Phone   **121**

Negotiating by correspondence   **121**

Negotiating by telephone   **124**

Key points   **125**

Chapter 16 - Handling the Media   **126**

Effective media communication   **127**

The choice of media and method   **128**

Press advertisements   128

Press releases   129

Press conferences   131

News stories   132

Media interviews   132

Key points   **135**

Chapter 17 - Influencing Managerial Negotiations   **136**

Status   **136**

Connections with sources of power   **139**

Obligations   **141**

The power of expertise   **143**

Key points   **144**

Chapter 18 - Influencing Commercial Negotiations   **146**

    Sales techniques   **147**

    General bargaining principles   **148**

    Contractual implications   **150**

    Key points   **151**

Chapter 19 - Influencing Negotiations with Trade Unions   **153**

    Personal relationships   **153**

    Procedures   **155**

    Precedents   **157**

    Trade union legislation   **159**

    Key points   **160**

Chapter 20 - Negotiating Skills   **162**

    Knowledge   **162**

    Skill 164

    Attitudes   **168**

The book is essentially practical in style and includes many case studies to illustrate the principles which are discussed. It is a text for managers of all disciplines - not only personnel managers – though personnel professionals should find much useful material about industrial relations bargaining. Teachers, trainers and students in personnel and general management should find the case studies of particular value.

Its underlying theme is that negotiation needs to be seen as a *constructive* process: a method of achieving effective results - not as a battle for the preservation of personal or corporate power and prestige.

Chapter 1 - Understanding Basic Principles

To most personnel managers, negotiation implies collective bargaining. To a sales executive, it will be thought of in terms of making a commercial deal. Quantity surveyors, purchasing managers and lawyers all have their own specialist interpretations of what, in essence, is a process common to all managerial work. For in reality, all managers negotiate, if not with outside parties then with each other.

The procedures and language of formal negotiation vary with the type of negotiation involved. A set-piece pay bargaining session has its own particular system and jargon which differ from those of a meeting of solicitors to settle a claim for libel damages. Yet the underlying principles and much of the psychology of the process is the same for all forms of negotiation.

It is also easy for managers to overlook the fact that much of their informal daily activity is, in effect, negotiation. All managers spend a large proportion of their time trying to influence and persuade other managers over whom they have no executive authority.

Consider two examples:

• A sales executive tries to persuade the production manager to change a manufacturing schedule to fit in a small order for a special customer. The production manager has full authority to decide production schedules against a weekly output plan set by top management. Officially, the sales manager should make a request through the sales director for an urgent variation to this plan but, because the order is only a small one, approaches the production manager informally and must, therefore, rely on persuasion.

• A personnel manager attempts to 'sell' the need for a more systematic form of employee consultation to a reluctant office manager. The company has a general policy of support for employee involvement practices, but has not laid down any specific system or procedure. Neither the extent to which the personnel manager can use the general policy to require the office manager's co-operation, nor the right of the office manager to reject the personnel manager's suggestions, are clearly defined. The outcome will be influenced by their possibly differing perceptions of the formal position, and on the powers of argument or persuasion of the personnel manager.

Negotiating skills are, therefore, a very important element in the effective manager's portfolio of personal competencies. Recognizing when negotiation is occurring is the first step, and this is aided by an understanding of the basic principles involved.

A definition

Negotiation is a process, not a single skill. A range of skills are involved in handling this process effectively, but to identify the skills which are relevant to any particular negotiating episode, it is important to recognize which elements or principles of negotiation are involved. There are seven principles common to all forms of negotiation:

• Negotiation involves two or more parties who need - or think they need - each other's involvement in achieving some desired outcome. There must be some common interest, either in the subject matter of the negotiation or in the negotiating context, which puts or keeps the parties in contact.

• While sharing a degree of interest, the parties start with different objectives, and these differences initially prevent the achievement of an outcome.

• At least initially, the parties consider that negotiation is a more satisfactory way of trying to resolve their differences than alternatives such as coercion or arbitration.

• Each party considers that there is some possibility of persuading the other to modify their original position. It is not essential - though it is usually highly desirable - for each party to be willing to compromise. But negotiation can begin when both parties have an initial intention of maintaining their opening positions: but each has some hope of persuading the other to change.
• Similarly, even when their ideal outcomes prove unattainable, both parties retain some hope of an acceptable final agreement.

• Each party has some influence or power - real or assumed – over the other's ability to act. If one party is entirely powerless, there may be no point in the other party committing itself to a negotiating process. The matter can be settled unilaterally by the party with the untrammelled power to act. This power or influence may, however, be indirect and bear on issues other than those which are the direct subject of negotiation.

• The negotiating process itself is one of interaction between people - in most cases by direct, verbal interchange. Even when the negotiation is being conducted through correspondence, there is an essential underlying human element. The progress of all types of negotiation is strongly influenced by emotion and attitudes, not just by the facts or logic of each party's arguments. Putting all these principles together, a definition emerges which provides a summary and a starting point for a detailed examination of the various parts of the process, and the strategies and skills involved:
Negotiation is a process of interaction by which two or more parties who consider they need to be jointly involved in an outcome, but who initially have different objectives, seek by the use of argument and persuasion to resolve their differences in order to achieve a mutually acceptable solution.

It will probably be readily accepted that this definition is relevant to formal negotiations such as pay bargaining, or the settlement of a legal claim for damages. Trade union and employer - or the solicitors representing two parties to litigation - obviously accept that they need jointly to evolve a mutually satisfactory outcome, starting from differing positions. Each party knows that the other has some power to influence the outcome. The trade union might apply the sanction of industrial action: the employer might reduce the labour force: the claimant's solicitors might stop negotiating and take the case to court: the respondent has some defence if this occurs. But how does the definition apply to the two examples given earlier of managers trying to persuade their colleagues to accept new courses of action?

The sales executive has no direct power to require the production manager to alter production schedules: the production manager can just say no - so where does negotiation come in? A willingness at least to consider the request - and thereby become involved in a discussion about a possible jointly satisfactory outcome - will stem from several aspects of common interest, or from a recognition of more subtle forms of power.

• The sales executive wants the production schedules altered, the production manager does not. but both managers, it is to be hoped, share an interest in the success of the business. To disappoint an important customer may be of more immediate concern to the sales executive than to the production manager, but a good production manager will pay heed to the importance of good customer service. Similarly, the sales executive will recognize the costs and perhaps delays to other orders that a change in the production schedule might give rise to. So a common interest in the good of the business enables both to see something in the other's point of view, and thus encourages a dialogue, rather than the simple exercise of formal authority.

• It may be that the sales executive (or the customer on whose behalf the request is being made) is known by the production manager to be highly regarded by the managing director. It might thus be unwise, in terms of company politics, for the production manager to run the risk of being considered unhelpful.

• Both managers also know that they have to continue to work together. Without anything being said. both will probably be influenced by knowing that this long-term working relationship could be adversely affected by mishandling the particular incident. The production manager may have the right to say no - in other words. not to negotiate - but will wonder whether this would cause avoidable friction. There may also be the thought that by agreeing some concession, an obligation may be created that might be capitalized on at some future date.

Considerations of a similar kind might also lead to the office manager being willing to discuss the personnel manager's advice. Both have an interest in the smooth running of the company and in compliance with company policy; the personnel manager may be known to have top management backing; the managers have to go on working together therefore the office manager will have to consider the implications of rejecting the personnel manager's advice if employee relations are then seen to deteriorate.

Negotiation and consultation

These examples illustrate situations in which, despite an uneven distribution of power, each party accepts either that the other has some right to influence the outcome, or that a jointly evolved solution is more desirable than an imposed one. It is not unusual, however, for managers to find themselves unexpectedly in a negotiating situation - often because they confuse consultation with negotiation. Consider this example:

Jane Tonbridge is the newly-appointed finance manager of a bus company. She decides to reorganize her department and is told by the chief executive that she has *carte blanche* to do so provided she avoids additional expenditure. He suggests, though. that she might care to have a chat with Bill Truscott, the long-serving operations manager. She draws up her plans for restructuring her department, sees Bill, tells him the plans, outlines their advantages as she sees them, and finishes by saying: 'I hope you agree.' Whereupon Bill ponders for a moment and then says: 'Sorry, but I don't. You would do better to keep things as they are.'

Jane now has an awkward choice. She can say in effect: 'I'm sorry about that - but it's my department and I was only sounding you out. not asking for your approval.' Alternatively, she can begin to argue the pros and cons of her and Bill's ideas. If she does this, which is clearly more tactful if less satisfactory to her than rebuffing Bill, she has begun negotiating.

Tacitly, she will be accepting a need to reach a conclusion which Bill accepts. This outcome may well be a very different reorganization than the one which ideally she would like.

What has gone wrong for lane is that a process she intended as consultation has been interpreted by the other party as an invitation to negotiate because of the way she approached the discussion. To achieve a true consultative approach, she should have seen Bill before finalizing her plans, saying something like: 'I'm looking at how my department operates: is there anything from your point of view which you think I should take into account?' This would leave her free to develop her own plans: it implies no commitment to accept any specific proposal by Bill: it does not place him in a position to express approval. It is genuine consultation.

The difference from negotiation is crucial, and can be summarized in two further definitions:

Negotiation implies acceptance by both parties that agreement between them is required (or is desirable) before a decision can be implemented.

Consultation implies a willingness by one party to listen to the views of the other, while reserving the right to make a final decision, whether or not the other party is in agreement.

Is negotiation necessary?

One aspect of effective negotiation is, therefore, to decide or recognize in advance, whether a particular interaction will require negotiation, or whether it can be kept at consultation.

Negotiation can be a lengthy process, and by asking whether it is necessary, time may sometimes be saved and unnecessary compromise avoided. On occasions, a request to negotiate may best be met by pointing out that the party making the request has no standing in the matter. If a manager has the undoubted authority to act, making a decision rather than negotiating about it may be the best tactic.

Alternatively, there are cases in which the best response to a request or a claim is to concede it without argument. Why waste time negotiating if the other party has a good case and there are no adverse consequences in conceding? Unnecessary negotiation, followed, perhaps, by a grudging concession of the other party's claim, will lose all the advantage which might be gained by a quick, unexpected 'Yes'.

An alternative to a simple Yes or No when a difference of view occurs is to skip negotiation and proceed immediately to some form of third party intervention. On the most formal basis, this might imply a decision to take a dispute to court: informally, two managers who quickly realize that they cannot reach agreement about a working problem may jointly agree to stop wasting time in argument and refer the matter to a senior manager for resolution.

A good general rule is: *don't* negotiate unless you have to – or unless you can obtain some direct or indirect advantage by doing so.

Stages in negotiation

Assuming negotiation is necessary or desirable, three stages need to be handled well:

• A preparation phase before the negotiation begins.
• The actual negotiating process - the interaction which leads to an agreement about an outcome.
• The implementation of the agreement (or agreement as to how the outcome is to be implemented) - a stage sometimes given too little attention because of a preoccupation with winning the negotiating arguments.

Preparation

Negotiations need to be planned, and several later chapters deal in detail with such aspects as assessing the relative strength of the parties and the setting of negotiating objectives. Two preliminary questions are useful:

• What are the real issues?
• Which parties should be involved?

The first question is often of particular importance in industrial relations, as the following example illustrates:

George Truscott was the regional personnel manager of an insurance company. The regional office had recently been reorganized, and several new, young section managers transferred in from other branches. Over a three-month period, the trade union representative of the premiums section brought a series of complaints to George about heating, lighting, the design of new office furniture and the new office layout. This culminated in a formal demand by the union for a meeting to discuss and resolve all these housekeeping issues.

George felt that other matters might lie behind this apparent general dissatisfaction with the physical aspects of the office, and that to attempt to negotiate just on these aspects might not improve matters. Instead of setting up a formal meeting, he, therefore, engineered an occasion to have an off-the-record and informal talk with the union representative.

From this conversation, it became evident that the real, though underlying issue was resentment by the premiums staff about the imposition, as they saw it, of a young, brash, uncommunicative manager from another branch. This indicated that a different negotiating strategy would have to be evolved - even though some aspects of housekeeping did need to be addressed.

The question as to which parties should be involved sometimes occurs in an industrial relations context, and frequently needs consideration when informal managerial negotiations take place. With trade unions, negotiations may occur with manual or production workers about changes in working practices. These changes may have an effect on the jobs of white-collar staff, and it has not been unknown for companies to conclude agreements with their manual trade unions before recognizing that parallel negotiations are necessary to secure the co-operation of the clerical or other support staff, Inadequate attention has been paid to the question of who needs to be involved.

Similar problems can occur when two managers meet to discuss an issue which is also of concern to a third. Thus, a change to factory maintenance schedules, agreed between a chief engineer and a production manager, may have implications for the stores operation which is managed by the purchasing manager. His omission from the discussion will probably mean that his initial reaction to the change will be unhelpful.

During negotiation

The whole negotiating process is dealt with in detail in succeeding chapters. Here, it is enough to note that most effective negotiations follow a six-stage pattern:

• The parties start by agreeing what it is they are negotiating about - they define the issues.
• Each side then sets out what it is seeking: or the side making a claim puts its case, and the other party gives an initial response they define their initial positions.
• There is then a more open phase when the initial positions are tested in argument.
• The parties then move to a tentative exploration of possible outcomes.
• Firm or formal proposals are then made, discussed and perhaps modified.
• Finally, an agreement is defined and concluded.

Implementation

Ill-defined agreements, or agreements which have paid too little attention to the practicalities of implementation, frequently collapse soon after they have been concluded. While the purpose of negotiation is to achieve an agreement, the purpose of an

agreement must be to implement some positive action. Three steps can help to prevent an implementation failure:
• In all but the more informal of negotiations, confirm what has been agreed in writing.
• If appropriate, include an implementation programme in the agreement. In other words, agree who is committed to doing what by when - don't leave this undefined to become the subject of later disagreement.
• Ensure everyone concerned is told about the agreement, what it implies, and the action which will follow. In many cases, the need for this information will be much wider than just the persons who took part in the actual negotiations.

Key points

• All managers negotiate - with each other, as well as with customers, suppliers, trade unions and other outside parties.
• Negotiation is about achieving a mutually acceptable outcome to a situation in which the parties involved initially have differing aims.
• Negotiations are affected by emotions and attitudes of the negotiators - not just by the logic of the arguments they use.
• Consultation needs to be distinguished from negotiation. In negotiation, the parties accept that joint agreement is necessary: in consultation, one party reserves the right to act unilaterally.
• Do not negotiate unless this is either necessary, or some advantage may be obtained by so doing.
• Three stages are involved: preparation, the negotiation itself, and implementation.

Chapter 2 - Weighing Relative Strengths

Before embarking on negotiation, it is important to assess the strength of each side's bargaining position. In an industrial relations context, this may mean considering whether, by taking industrial action, the trade union could prevent the implementation of the employer's proposals. On the union side, an assessment may be made of the likelihood of the employer obtaining an injunction to prevent industrial action. In a more informal managerial situation, factors such as the extent to which a manager's proposals are backed by company policy or by the availability of resources will affect the assessment. Being in a strong bargaining position implies that one has more power than the other party to influence the outcome in the direction one prefers.

The exercise of this power is often more indirect than industrial or legal action. Negatively, it may consist of generating inconvenience through delays - a not uncommon feature of legal negotiations – or of creating an unpleasant or irritating working relationship. In a positive sense, it implies that one party can offer more advantage or benefit in support of its case than the other. It is rare for an assessment of relative strength to be capable of precise calculation, or to be reduced to a simple arithmetical calculation. It is normally a matter of judgement in which at least four forms of power or influence are involved:

• The degree of authority or ability each party has to make and implement decisions about the matter in question.
• The ability of each party to influence the other through some form of sanction or benefit which may be unrelated to the matter under negotiation.
• The strength of the arguments in favour of each party's case in terms of logic or equity.
• The determination with which each party pursues its case.

Two examples can be used to illustrate how assessments of each of these aspects may influence negotiating strategy:

• Jill Wright is the advertising sales manager for a computer journal. Her job is to maximize income from the sale of advertising space to computer and software suppliers. She knows she could sell more space if the journal ran major articles, planned several months in advance, on topics suggested by advertisers and to which their advertisements could be related.

Gordon Derbyman is the editor. His policy is to work to short time-scales to ensure the news value of articles and thereby attract and hold a volatile readership. He is not keen on advertisement-linked features.
Gordon and Jill are of equal managerial status: both report to a managing director who oversees four other technical journals and whose policy is to give the editors full control over journal content. Jill wants to persuade Gordon to run at least one major quarterly article to which additional advertising can be linked.
She is now considering how best to obtain Gordon's agreement.

• A local Council has decided to move all its currently scattered services to a new, central office block. The director of administration, Ronald Morris, has the responsibility for planning this move and has the executive authority to decide the necessary allocation of office space.
He knows that whichever detailed office plan he prepares it will be unpopular with one or other of the departments to be moved. They all value their current separate office identities.
They are all determined to secure the most favoured office areas in the new block.
Having prepared what is, in his view, the most efficient office plan, Ronald has convened a meeting of the heads of the departments affected by the move. He has told them that the aim of the meeting is 'to attempt to reach a mutually acceptable allocation of office space in the new HQ' and is now planning his tactics for the meeting.

These two examples can now be examined against the four aspects of negotiating strength outlined above.

Decision-making power

In the first example, Jill (the manager wishing to achieve change) has no direct authority or decision-making power. Gordon, the editor, is able simply to reject her suggestion. In contrast, Ronald in the second example has the authority, if he wishes, to impose his office plan on the other departmental heads - though he has chosen to attempt a negotiated solution. In each case - though for opposite reasons - negotiation could have been a non-starter. To be successful in their negotiations, both need to recognize this possibility and plan accordingly.

In Jill's case, if she gives any impression that she is challenging or is resentful of Gordon's editorial authority, she will run the risk of him reverting to the role of autocratic editor and refusing to listen to her ideas. She must search for other forms of influence.

Ronald could have chosen not to negotiate. He is attempting this course, however, mainly because he would prefer to implement a plan which the departmental heads have accepted, rather than use his authority to override their probable objections. In handling the meeting he would be wise, though, not to appear to have surrendered this authority. He may need to remind the other managers, if the going gets rough, that if they cannot agree he will have no option but to impose his own plan. Part of his negotiating strategy, therefore, is to make positive use of his decision-making power, without necessarily having directly to exercise it.

In conventional collective bargaining such as an annual pay negotiation, it is tacitly accepted that each party will suspend its powers of unilateral action while the negotiation proceeds. Yet both parties will be influenced by their separate assessments of their relative strengths. Similarly, when purchasing managers are negotiating prices with suppliers, both are influenced by their views on the extent to which the buyer might be able to obtain the goods from an alternative source. The buyer of a unique but essential product is in an exceedingly weak bargaining position - and will consequently wish, if at all possible, to conceal this dependency from the single supplier.

The power of influence

Negotiators are often influenced by considerations other than the pros and cons of the matter under discussion. It is under this heading that Jill, in particular, will need to plan her case. Can Gordon's likely opposition to her request be modified by other factors which he will perceive as offering benefits or carrying risks? This is where office politics sometimes intrude. If Jill thinks she is in better standing than Gordon with the managing director she may be able to imply that rejection of her request might be viewed with disfavour. However, using actual or implied threats of this kind is a risky tactic which may generate resentment and obstruction. People respond more favourably to benefits than threats: as the American sales trainers say, 'sell it sunny side up'. So Jill's ploy is to remind
Gordon that under company policy, extra advertising pages will allow him more editorial space, to portray her quarterly advertisement -linked articles as an extra feature - not as an erosion of current editorial content - and to point out the interest to readers, not just to advertisers, of what she has in mind.

Ronald can afford to be much less concerned with his ability to influence. He can plan his negotiations against a background of ultimate authority and on the logic of his plans. He may, nevertheless, think about the advantage he may gain for the future by giving the departmental heads this opportunity to influence the office plans. Among those affected is the director of finance. Ronald knows that this director is working on a new system for costing and allocating office overheads. This new system will affect Ronald's budget, and could be imposed by the finance director. Perhaps, thinks Ronald, by avoiding the imposition of the office plan, he can put some credit 'in the bank' with the finance director and that this may lead to a discussion of the new costing system, rather than its imposition. More generally, he knows that all the managers will appreciate being given the opportunity of reaching a corporate agreement, and this will benefit the whole of his working relationship with them.

In managerial and trade union negotiations, their effect on long-term relationships is often an influential, if indirect factor. A purchasing manager may adopt an aggressive attitude in negotiating with a possible supplier, knowing that if the bargaining fails, the relationship ends. But two managers, or a manager and a shop steward, know that they have to maintain working contacts regardless of the outcome of anyone negotiating episode. Consciously or unconsciously, they may moderate their bargaining positions to avoid damaging their long-term relationship.

The strength of the case

None of these more general considerations of power and influence should divert the negotiators' attention from the efficacy of their specific arguments and objectives. There is certainly a risk that too great an emphasis on the 'political' dimension will result in a bad decision about the issue under negotiation.

Jill must clearly rely mainly on the strength of her proposals in sound business terms. This means she must have all the evidence available to support her arguments - market trends, advertiser and reader responses, the practice of competitors and cost and profit forecasts. The weaker the power position, the stronger the detailed case needs to be.

Ronald, too, needs to be able to show that he has recognized the departmental heads' needs and produced a solution which, while not satisfying all their separate objectives, produces a reasonable balance which makes overall sense. One of his reasons for deciding to negotiate rather than dictate is that he has realized that almost every feature of his plan that will be objected to by one manager, will be to another's advantage. His strategy, therefore, is not to set himself up against a united front of objectors, but to use their separate and differing views to counter each other's arguments. He is confident that by highlighting these differences, the logic of his own plan will emerge.

An example of the power of the arguments used in support of a case for local authority manual workers:

Pay levels for this group of nearly one million employees had been deteriorating for several years and the unions submitted a large, 'catching up' claim. The employers' willingness to do much about this was severely limited by the reductions central government were making in local government grants and the employers' opening position was: 'We're sorry, but we haven't got the money.' The trade unions were thought to be in a very weak position. Much of their membership consisted of women in part-time jobs - not a group likely to support industrial action. There were also fears of redundancy caused by the government's tight financial constraints.

The unions' negotiating strategy had, therefore, to be based wholly on the strength of their case. As the leading union negotiator later explained: "We set out to establish the case, making the employers feel embarrassed at paying such low rates." A detailed statistical analysis was presented to the employers, backed by very skilful and emotional appeals about the hardships being suffered by loyal hardworking but low-paid employees. The unions eventually won a much higher settlement than the employers initially said they could afford, plus a beneficial re-evaluation of all jobs the following year. What undermined the employers' original resolve was not the unions' industrial strength but the sheer weight of logic in the claim. and the appeal to the employers' sense of fairness.

Determination

Negotiations are influenced by the determination or persistence of the parties. This was one of the features of the unions' tactics in the pay negotiations described above. The simple message that it was unfair for so many employees to be so low paid was hammered home on every possible occasion - not just in the formal negotiating sessions but in informal contacts between union officials and employers, and through media statements and interviews. Initial resistance to a proposal or claim can sometimes be worn down by persistence.

This can be seen, for example, in claims for compensation made by holiday-makers against travel companies and reported by the Consumers Association. The claimant's case is often initially rejected, or only nominal payment offered. But a persistent claimant - negotiating through correspondence and telephone or perhaps using the threat of legal action - often achieves a higher negotiated settlement.

This is a factor which Jill will need to keep in mind. Her first approach to Gordon may be unsuccessful. If she thinks this is likely, her strategy might include being ready to try again, perhaps with her arguments recast, and with some extra features which she can use to justify her persistence.

There is an important difference between determination and a stubborn refusal to compromise. Most negotiations involve some give and take on both sides. To persist in a refusal to alter one's opening position may achieve no more than a breakdown in negotiation.

Lord Goodman, the internationally renowned lawyer, was once asked what he considered to be the single most important quality of the effective negotiator. He replied: 'The determination to achieve an agreement' - not, it will be noted, a determination never to compromise.

Key points

• Before embarking on negotiation there is a need to assess the parties' relative strengths.
• Strength is the power or influence each can exercise over the final outcome.
• Power and influence may be indirect, affecting factors other than the immediate issues under negotiation.
• It may take four forms:

- decision-making authority
- the power of influence
- the strength of the actual case
- the determination or persistence of the negotiator.

• Influence may be negative - causing the other party damage: or positive - offering the other party benefit or advantage.

• The strength of the actual case can include its logical validity and its emotional appeal.

Chapter 3 - Setting the Objectives

In planning a negotiation, an assessment of relative strength needs to be linked to the determination of objectives - the outcomes which are aimed for. To a large extent, the stronger one's position, the higher or more optimistic can be the objective.

Commercial negotiators are often advised to define three possible settlement levels:

• The ideal, or best possible deal
• The expected settlement level
• The worst, though still just acceptable deal.

So a stationery supplier, negotiating next year's supply contract with a major customer, might set a figure of £150,000 as the ideal objective, £140,000 as a more realistic expected outcome, and £120,000 as the bottom line.
Meanwhile the buyer might be setting £100,000 as the ideal price, £115,000 as the expected outcome and £130,000 as the outside limit.
Assuming no other factors intrude, the logic of these figures is that the final settlement will fall between £120,000 and £130,000 - the overlap between the two parties' ranges of objectives.
This form of analysis provides a starting point for considering objectives, but it is much too simplistic for many negotiations. In real life, things are rarely as clear cut, with other factors than price influencing the outcome and with both parties aware of alternatives.
An example illustrates this:

Sue Downs is the computer manager for a retail group. She is about to negotiate with a software company, for the supply of a computerized personnel records system. None of the packages on the market meet all her needs, but the software company have a package which, with some modifications, would be close to ideal. A technically similar package might be developed by another software house, but they have quoted nine months for design and delivery. Sue wants a system up and running well before then.

She has a budget of £25.000 to cover the purchase of the new system and initial staff training. If the cost is less? The saving can be carried over to next year for further computer enhancement. If the cost is higher, she will either have to make offsetting savings elsewhere in her department or seek top management approval to exceed her budget.

Price is not the only factor she has to take into account.

Delivery dates are important and ideally she would like the system operational within two months: six months is her outside limit. She could compromise a little on technical specification if this eased any price or delivery problems. She has a choice, too, of negotiating for training to be done by the software company as part of a turnkey deal, or of handling training herself.

Two non-financial factors also affect her analysis of objectives. Next year, she has it in mind to make a case for upgrading her company's mainframe computer. If at all possible, therefore, she not only wants to avoid going to top management for a budget overspend this year, she would like to accumulate a budget surplus to help in arguing her case next year. Against this, the personnel and finance managers are pressing very hard to have a new records system installed as quickly as possible.

They are already expressing criticism of the delay caused by her very thorough exploration of the software market.

Thus in deciding the upper and lower limits for the outcome of her negotiation. Sue has to use her judgement - not just a statistical calculation - to balance a quite complex interaction between:

1 price

2 delivery

3 specification
- system features
- training

4 relationships
- with top management
- with colleagues

She also has to consider the bargaining strength of the supplier and to set all this against an alternative of dropping the software company, changing the outside limit on delivery, and approaching the alternative supplier.

Deciding the top line

For many negotiations in which more complex issues exist than the single factor of price, it is more useful to identify a 'best achievable' top line than try to distinguish between an ideal and an expected outcome. This is the best outcome it is realistic to expect to achieve having taken all factors into account including relative strength. It might well consist of a set of alternatives. In Sue's case, for example, there may be several permutations of price, delivery and specification which would all be fully satisfactory.

The most common failing in planning for negotiation is over optimism about this achievable outcome. In negotiations with trade unions, for example, there is a tendency for managers to convince themselves that they have an unarguable case - based on business logic - for offering only a very modest pay rise; and that the unions will reluctantly accept this without resorting to any form of industrial action. A 'final offer' is eventually made, with managers confident of acceptance. Frustratingly, the unions then refuse to accept what managers felt was the overwhelming evidence to support the finality of the offer, and persist in pressing a higher claim - backed, perhaps, by strike action.

Similar over-optimism often infects other forms of negotiation. The personnel manager assumes the office manager will agree to a new method of employee consultation because, from a personnel viewpoint, the new system is obviously better. A supplier assumes the customer will not object too strongly to a price increase because the product has obviously been improved. A chief executive is convinced that the company need pay only a very modest sum in a negotiated settlement for an unfair dismissal because to think otherwise would be admitting a greater degree of company blame than he is prepared to consider.

There is a common thread running through all these examples – a failure to consider the position from the other party's point of view. In pay negotiations, managers need to ask themselves how the union officials will justify a low pay settlement to their union members. The personnel manager needs to assess what the advantages of the new consultation system are from the production manager's viewpoint.

The supplier should consider whether the product improvements are so relevant to the customer that they will overcome resistance to the price increase. The chief executive needs to look at the dismissal from the standpoint of the employee concerned.

The bottom line

Over-optimism about probable outcome is often linked with a failure to give adequate consideration to the bottom line - the worst outcome which would still just be acceptable. This failure carries two risks:
• An over-rigid position will be taken by refusing to compromise or to consider alternative outcomes. A damaging breakdown in negotiations may then occur.
• Alternatively, once the ideal outcome has been shown to be unrealistic or unattainable, no prepared fall-back position has been identified, and an eventual agreement may be concluded which is worse than circumstances justify.
In many cases, identifying the bottom line is more important than setting the original target. There may be a variety of possible satisfactory outcomes, so that flexibility in setting the best achievable target is essential. But there are usually some elements (costs, prices, standards) which must be set as outside, lower limits. In the software negotiations used as an earlier example, Sue might well decide that the total cost - whatever the precise package - must not exceed £28,000 and the outside limit for delivery is six months. Any package deal on which one or both of these limits is exceeded must be rejected.
Being clear about the bottom line is a necessary protection against being persuaded, in the heat of negotiations, to accept outcomes which inflict real damage, and which are worse in their effect than the breakdown in negotiations which might occur if the bottom line is held.

Credibility

It is obviously unwise to declare one's upper and lower limits when negotiations begin. The other party would then ignore the top line and concentrate on negotiating down to the bottom limit as quickly as possible. In any event, some flexibility needs to be maintained, particularly during the joint exploration of possible outcomes. Unforeseen points or proposals may be raised which will require a quick reconsideration of one's limits. In Sue's case, for example, the supplier might offer a leasing deal instead of outright purchase, or might suggest staging payments over a three-year period. In both cases, a new bottom line would be worth consideration.

There may come a point, however, when a decision and a statement needs to be made about this outside limit, such as: 'I cannot in any circumstances go beyond £28,000.' Or in a trade union negotiation:

'6 per cent plus one day's extra leave has to be our final offer.'

If credibility is to be sustained, final must *mean* final. Companies have often undermined their own negotiating position by ill prepared, over-hasty or too frequent declarations that the bottom line has been reached, only to be forced by circumstances to waive this limit and agree to further concessions. Statements about limits being reached, or about items being non-negotiable, need to be made with care and only in circumstances where the line can actually be held.

Winning and losing

It is common parlance to describe negotiations in terms of winning or losing. Popular media coverage often portrays the final outcome of an industrial dispute as being a victory for one side or the other and rarely as a balanced compromise with benefits to both sides. Yet many writers and trainers urge negotiators to adopt a 'win/win' strategy. By this they mean attempting to reach agreements in which both parties feel they have achieved an advantageous outcome - as distinct from a 'win/lose' approach in which each party sets out to defeat the other. In a win/win strategy, negotiation is seen as a collaborative, rather than combative process.

This is a valuable attitude to adopt, particularly where negotiations are between people or institutions which have a long-term working relationship - such as employer and trade union, or between managers in the same organization. The damage to an important working contact which can be caused by one unpleasantly adversarial bout of win/lose negotiation can be considerable.

It has to be recognized, however, that a genuine win/win strategy can be pursued only when both parties adopt this approach. Unfortunately for the theorists, many negotiators – particularly those who have not had the benefit of win/win training - see negotiation as a competitive, if not combative, process. An aggressive, but adept negotiator will quickly take advantage of the good faith and helpfulness of an unwary or naive win/win protagonist.

There are also occasions when one party takes a wholly unacceptable position or presses a highly damaging claim, but circumstances prevent an outright rejection or a cessation of negotiation. In such cases there may be little alternative but to adopt a vigorous and assertive negotiating posture, and attempt to undermine the other side's position. This does not imply the adoption of an unpleasantly antagonistic personal manner: it does involve a determination not to be trampled on and not to allow the other side, in effect, to win.

It is for these practical reasons that later chapters of this book include a few tactics, or responses to aggressive negotiation, which not all win/win theorists would be enthusiastic about.

Key points

- Negotiators need to identify a top line objective - the best achievable outcome: and a bottom line - the lowest, still acceptable outcome.
- Over-optimism about the probable outcome is often linked to a failure to consider the bottom line.
- Top and bottom lines may each consist of several alternative permutations of the issues under negotiation.
- Possible outcomes need to be considered from the other party's viewpoint as well as one's own.
- It is important to retain credibility by restricting statements about 'final offers' or sticking points to *genuine* bottom lines.
- If possible, one objective should be to help the other party to feel satisfied with the outcome; but an aggressive or damaging claim has to be resisted with vigour.

Chapter 4 - Assessing the Other Side's Case

Subjecting one's own case to critical scrutiny and deciding objectives and limits does not complete the preparation for a negotiating episode. It is also important to obtain as much information as possible about the position to be taken by the other party. Three main points are involved:

• What the other party is aiming for and their likely negotiating limits.
• The facts and arguments they are likely to use to support their case.
• Whether there are any underlying and unstated issues or objectives, i.e. a hidden agenda.

An industrial relations example can be used to illustrate these points:

George, the personnel manager of an engineering company, received a letter from Harry, the Union district organizer. The Union represented the company's maintenance workers who included a small building section, responsible for repairs to factory buildings. Harry's letter -which had been addressed to the chief executive who passed it on - asked for an urgent meeting 'to resolve the unsatisfactory position arising from the use by the company of subcontractors to undertake repairs to the roof of Block A'. George knew that the maintenance shop steward was alleging that the subcontractors were in breach of building safety regulations, and that there was bad feeling between the maintenance employees and the subcontractor's workforce. George thought the problem might also be that the subcontractor's employees were not union members, though it was not clear from Harry's letter just what the Union would be seeking in any meeting.

George, therefore, replied to the Union letter, saying that the chief executive had a heavy diary and that it would help to speed the matter if Harry could provide a note of the particular issues he wished to discuss. This produced a phone call from Harry, from which it was evident that the complaint was that the maintenance section thought they could have done the roof repairs - probably on overtime - and objected to 'their work' being put out to contract. Overtime earnings loomed large in Harry's conversation.

Discovering the other party's aims

It is helpful in any type of negotiation, formal or informal, to know in advance what the other party wants to discuss and in broad terms, what they are aiming for. In commercial negotiations this may generally be obvious - a meeting set up specifically, say, to negotiate an office rent review or to attempt to agree a price for some new equipment.

In many other negotiations, including informal inter-managerial episodes, the issue at stake may not become evident to the responding party until the discussion actually begins. This means that the party initiating the discussion has a marked advantage. He or she has been able to prepare a case: the other party has to respond without preparation. In the trade union example, George knows that Harry is an assertive and well-prepared negotiator. He does not want to be caught on the hop by being faced with an unexpected and perhaps well-documented claim - hence his follow-up suggestion to Harry before a meeting is fixed. This showed that earnings and job demarcation were the prime issues - not safety nor union membership – and George can now ensure that he is fully briefed on what will be the substance of any negotiations. He can make a reasonable assumption that the union's main aims will be protection of earnings and jobs.

The same principles can apply to a much more informal situation:

A typical managerial episode started with a line manager telephoning the purchasing manager and saying: 'May I come and see you about the policy on replacing office equipment?' Actually, the line manager had seen a new desk advertised and wanted to persuade the purchasing manager to buy one. Instead of just agreeing to the meeting, the purchasing manager said: 'What particular aspect of the policy do you want to talk about. Is there anything specific you want to discuss?' It then became evident that the line manager's real aim was to have a new and better desk - regardless of any policy. This gave the purchasing manager the choice of preparing a response to the particular request if there was scope for discussion; or to save time by giving an immediate Yes or No.

There is a tendency for managers with a very specific problem or request to wrap this up in a general enquiry about policy or procedure. Personnel managers, for example, are used to other managers asking for a generalized interpretation of company policy on employee discipline, when what they really want to negotiate is legitimacy for a specific dismissal. A failure by the personnel manager to flush out the real case can lead to serious difficulties. A general interpretation is given to an apparently general enquiry: a dismissal occurs which is then the subject of legal challenge: the line manager says that the action was taken on the personnel manager's advice: the personnel manager then realizes that if the initial, general enquiry had been probed, a specific case would have been identified to which the generalized advice was not wholly appropriate.
The better response to the first enquiry would have been: 'It's difficult to give you a general answer that would fit all cases: what's your particular problem?'

The other side's facts and arguments

Checking precisely what the issue is which the other party wants to pursue is only part of the preparation. It is even more helpful to know about the detailed facts and arguments they are likely to use, though this advantage is not necessarily one-way. In large, set-piece pay bargaining, it is not uncommon for the parties to exchange detailed written case statements, setting out the statistical and other evidence on which their claims and positions are based. Each side takes the view that the other party can be influenced before the negotiations begin by seeing the strength of a well-researched and prepared case. Both parties want to avoid the confusion which can occur during negotiations if a mass of detailed statistics are introduced in a piecemeal way.

In less complex or more informal negotiations, this advance tabling of supporting data is very unusual. It is therefore helpful, having established what the issue is, to consider what facts and arguments the other party has, or is likely to advance, in support of their case. For George, in the trade union example, this means examining trends in the maintenance employees' overtime working and earnings, and any precedents which the union might quote about the allocation of repair work to subcontractors.

As with all preparatory assessments, it is important to look at the situation from the other party's viewpoint as well as from one's own.

The question George should ask himself is: 'If I were Harry, what facts could I obtain to support my case, and how would I best use these in argument?' In the manual workers' pay bargaining example quoted in chapter two, the employers paid too little heed, before negotiating, to a range of uncomfortable facts about comparative pay trends (the basis of the unions' case) and relied too much on their own statistics about their limited financial resources. It is a common failing to think that one's own evidence is irrefutable and so to ignore or underestimate the conflicting data which the other party is bound to use.

A hidden agenda

Even after flushing out and assessing the specific issues to be dealt with and the data which supports the other party's case, there may still, in some circumstances, be an underlying issue which will affect the quality and outcome of the negotiations. So, a standard question should be: 'Are there any other issues which explain or will influence the way the other party will develop their case?'

This was a factor in George's case. The first letter from the union came from Harry, the full-time district official, to the chief executive.

This was 'unusual. Normally, Harry would be brought in only after the shop steward had exhausted discussions with George; normally, Harry's first contact would be with George - not with the chief executive. What lay behind Harry's departure from the normal procedure? It eventually transpired that the shop steward had reported to Harry that there had been a breakdown of mutual respect between George and the maintenance section. Harry's unorthodox letter to the chief executive was the opening shot in a fairly subtle union campaign to 'do something' about George.

Hidden agenda items also occur in commercial negotiations. A company negotiating an office cleaning contract with a local authority may have its sights set on a later, larger street cleaning contract, and may, consequently, see the smaller contract almost as a loss leader. An office equipment supplier, negotiating for the sale of photo-copiers, may be more interested in the longer run in obtaining a contract for the supply of stationery.

In managerial negotiations, other issues such as future relationships, later plans, personal prestige and rivalry frequently lie just beneath the surface. Check questions here, when approached by another manager with a proposal or request are: 'Why is this particular issue being raised at this time in this way? Is the issue being raised to make a point about some other matter? What else might this manager be seeking than just the satisfactory resolution of the issue under direct discussion?' These questions may seem to be negative and suspicious, but their intent is not to prevent a constructive resolution of the topics being debated. Rather, it is to ensure that the agreed solutions are not unwittingly biased by peripheral or unconnected factors.

Key points

• Establish what the other party's case is and what they are seeking to achieve.
• Probe whether specific problems or cases lie behind generalized questions or claims.
• Exchange factual data in advance of negotiations if this may helpfully influence the outcome or prevent delay and confusion during negotiation.
• Consider what facts and arguments the other party is likely to use in support of their case.
• Consider the possible existence of a hidden agenda - underlying issues which may influence the conduct and outcome of the negotiations.

Chapter 5 - Setting the Style and Scene

Having weighed up the bargaining position, set objectives, and assessed the nature of the other party's case, attention can now be turned to the more detailed planning of the actual negotiation. An important issue is the general style or tone to be adopted – discursive or brisk, formal or informal, assertive or persuasive. The extent to which one party can set the style and the physical arrangements (room layout, seating plan and the like) depends on which side is taking the initiative, and whether the other party is giving equal consideration to such planning. There has to be a good deal of flexibility in these preparations to cope with the possibility that the other party has planned a very different approach. However, many negotiators seem to pay relatively little attention to such factors, thus handing an advantage to the minority who do. Six aspects generally need consideration, though some are of more relevance to formal negotiations between teams than to informal discussions between individual managers. These points are:

- The style or tone of the negotiations
- Who to involve - the composition of the negotiating teams
- The pace or timing of the negotiation
- The location - 'their place or ours?'
- Seating arrangements and the provision of refreshments
- How the negotiation is to be documented

The style or tone

If both parties adopt the win/win approach which was discussed in the previous chapter, the style or tone of the negotiations will be firm but friendly, collaborative and constructive. Unless the other party is known to adopt aggressive tactics, an emphasis on joint problem solving rather than on winning debating points is by far the most effective. It would be very pleasant if it could be assumed that this style was universally adopted and, therefore, always appropriate.

In reality, no such assumption can be made. There are circumstances in which other styles are needed. Consider this example:

Memorex is a computer bureau which has a three year contract to provide a 'staff wages and costing system for Doublegee – a glazing company. The contract has been running for ten months. Doublegee recently wrote to Memorex, terminating the contract forthwith on the grounds that the system was failing to perform to specification. Memorex challenged this: there had been a few minor problems but no serious breakdown.

Memorex have heard on the industry grapevine that Doublegee have financial problems and are planning to cut their labour force and revert to a manual wages system. Memorex now submit a written claim for compensation for breach of contract. Doublegee counter-claim for alleged costs caused by system failures.

A meeting is arranged at Doublegee's offices with a view to reaching an agreed settlement. Given the tone of previous correspondence and telephone conversations, the Memorex team are not wholly surprised that the meeting starts with Doublegee's managing director launching an unpleasantly aggressive attack on Memorex's competence, tabling what he claims is chapter and verse for a string of system failures, and saying that unless Memorex drop their claim, he will pursue his counterclaim through the courts with technical evidence that will damage Memorex's professional reputation.

In planning for this negotiation, the Memorex team needs to prepare for just such an aggressive opening. They should avoid being provoked into an abusive rejoinder, but need to establish very quickly that they have a strong case and are not going to be bounced into surrendering their claim. Their best response is probably to call Doublegee's bluff by saying that Doublegee's statement is an ultimatum, not a negotiable proposal, and that unless Doublegee are prepared to discuss the whole position constructively there is no point in proceeding with the meeting. A less dramatic and more normal situation, particularly with discussions between managers and when negotiating with non-professionals such as shop stewards, is that the negotiation can go either way - constructive or combative - depending very much on the tone of the first few minutes. In these circumstances, the skilled negotiator always aims for a collaborative approach, and deliberately breaks the ice by a few minutes friendly general small talk before opening up the subject for discussion.

Who to involve

Informal managerial negotiations are normally between single individuals, not teams. Yet one-to-one bargaining has its drawbacks, particularly if one manager is a markedly more dominant personality than the other, or has significantly more negotiating experience. In such cases, the less confident manager should think of involving an additional person.

Leo, a young and recently appointed personnel manager, wanted to talk to May - a cynical, 55 year old divisional head - to persuade her to try using psychometric tests in the selection of graduate trainees. Leo had already had one very unsatisfactory talk with May on another topic in which his ideas had been swept aside with little discussion. This time, when ringing May to make a date for their discussion about tests, he added: 'I'll bring Bert Robinson with me - he can help us with the information about costs.' Bert was one of Leo's section heads, and the real and effective reason for this involvement was to reduce the dominance May could achieve in a one-to-one discussion.

In industrial relations, it is not uncommon for the trade union side to field a sizeable team - a union official, perhaps, supported by a shop stewards' committee. It is unwise for a single manager to attempt to negotiate alone with such a team. Negotiation demands a high level of concentration and quick thinking and it is difficult for one person to maintain full attention to everything that is said, and to detect every nuance in the discussion. This does not mean that the management team must equal the trade union team in size. Indeed, to go beyond a fairly small number runs the risk of poor co-ordination between team members and the possibility that differing views will emerge within the team as negotiations proceed. Many experienced negotiators express a preference for three members in a team, and certainly not more than five.

The composition of a team is also important. If difficulties are expected, it may be advisable to be ready to handle the negotiation on a staged basis. In wage bargaining, for example, the management team might consist, in the first instance, of the personnel manager, supported by two of his or her staff. If an impasse is reached, a second, higher level team may then be used consisting, perhaps, of the managing director, the finance director and the personnel manager. At least one person should be involved in both stages to ensure continuity and to prevent the other side misquoting things said at the first stage.

Within the team, thought needs to be given to each person's role.

In a team of three, for example:
• One will act as leader and take a constructive, problem-solving stance.
• Another will take a harder line, challenging the other party's assertions and generally pointing out the difficulties caused by their claims.
• The third member can act as 'sweeper', observing the reactions of the other team, checking progress, and bringing in any points missed by the other two members.

Pace and timing

The timing and pace of negotiation can have a major influence on the outcome. If a dispute has blown up very quickly about an issue on which emotions run high - such as a fatal accident at work – it may be as well to slow the pace of discussions to allow time for a highly-charged atmosphere to moderate. Achieving some delay in such circumstances requires very delicate handling. It is all too easy for a dispute on one issue (such as safety regulations) to be converted into a second dispute about the management's alleged time wasting or reluctance to talk. One way of proceeding is to suggest to the other party that a fact-finding exercise would be of use to both sides before formal negotiations begin.

In other circumstances, delay may increase the cost of the final settlement. This is particularly the case in wage bargaining during a period in which inflation is rising. Early in 1989, several companies achieved quick settlements by immediate offers of 6 per cent (considered high at the time) while others, who opened their offers at 4'12 per cent and were then bogged down in protracted bargaining, ended by paying 8 per cent or 9 per cent when inflation overtook their original positions.

Similar principles apply in commercial and managerial bargaining. It has become a well-established ploy in civil actions for compensation or damages for the lawyers to enter into protracted correspondence before any effective bargaining occurs about out-of-court settlements.

The theory is that the claimants will become so frustrated by lengthy delays that they will eventually agree to a much more modest settlement - simply to bring the matter to a conclusion - than they initially thought acceptable. The morality of such a tactic is obviously questionable. It may be, too, that far from weakening the resolve of the claimant, blatant time-wasting may strengthen his or her determination to succeed.

Although deciding on a slow or fast pace is a matter for judgment in each case, one general guideline can be suggested. It is to move quickly rather than slowly when the other party's position is a strong one. Indeed, at the extreme, there may be a case for conceding a claim or request without negotiation if the other party's argument cannot sensibly be challenged. Some managers resist any claim by a trade union as a matter of reactive routine. They would gain more respect if on occasions, when the union's proposal was clearly well-founded, they said Yes quickly and cheerfully - rather than being dragged to an eventual reluctant acceptance after time-wasting negotiation.

Location

There is often a choice of location for a negotiating meeting. For example, between managers or companies, in whose office should the meeting be held? Should a negotiating session with trade unions be held in the management offices or on neutral ground such as a hotel conference suite?
With experienced negotiators, location should make no difference, but for many people, the negotiating environment can influence their confidence and attitudes. This does not imply that given a choice, it is always best to select home territory.

A very experienced personnel manager in a large company was renowned for his persuasive ability in meetings with his managerial colleagues. Explaining his working methods to a new secretary. he said: 'Whenever I have meetings with other managers. however junior. I always try to hold them in their offices. not mine. It makes them feel I have put myself out a bit. and shown more of an interest in them. So I start one up!'

When the negotiations involve complex issues, it may be helpful to hold them on home ground so as to have ready access to supporting documents and possibly to call in additional team members as the discussions progress. Certainly, when such negotiations are located away from base, very careful thought needs to be given to the composition of the team and what files should be taken.

Large-scale, set-piece pay bargaining is often conducted on neutral ground to avoid any inference of advantage being gained by one side 'owning' the location. Even at a less formal level, it may be a good move to ask the union side if they would like the meeting held elsewhere than on the company's premises. It demonstrates an open, even-handed approach - and the outcome is quite likely to be a union suggestion to use the company's conference room.

Seating and refreshments

The seating plan for a negotiation can influence or reflect the participants' attitudes quite markedly. At its simplest, discussions between people sitting opposite each other at a very wide table tend to be more confrontational than if they are sitting next to each other in an informal group.

The conventional layout for a formal bargaining session is the 'across-the-table' format. Each team takes one side, with the two parties' leaders sitting directly opposite each other in the centres of the two long sides of the table. It is a format which many people feel comfortable with, because it emphasizes the separate identity of each side, and each has its own territory. On the other hand, it encourages a competitive us and them style, and is consequently not the best format for a negotiation in which one objective is to break down unnecessary attitudinal barriers between those involved.

For the more informal, collaborative approach, a round table is far better - or even a grouping of comfortable armchairs around a low table.

Ed, the personnel manager referred to in the last example, also explained to his new secretary how he liked to arrange the few meetings he held in his own office. 'If I'm telling someone rather than asking: he said, 'I stay behind my desk. Otherwise I always take them over to the coffee table, and put them in the deepest. softest armchair. It's very difficult to be belligerent when you are sunk into the upholstery, holding a cup of coffee.'

Occasionally, even in formal meetings, an unconventional seating plan may be contrived.

In one union negotiation, the management knew that the union official would take an aggressive line, while the senior shop steward was known to be much more conciliatory.
Letting the union team sit down first. the management leader then chose a chair at the table immediately opposite the senior steward, instead of in the centre facing the union official.
In the ensuing negotiation, the union official frequently had difficulty in catching the management leader's eye, while the latter was able to bring the senior steward into the discussion far more easily than if a conventional seating plan had been adopted.

The party hosting the negotiations (or taking the lead in organizing them if they are held on neutral territory) is expected to make some arrangements for refreshments. Providing tea and coffee, or beer and sandwiches, is an integral part of the formal negotiating ritual. Even when two managers are meeting informally, for the 'host' to omit to offer a cup of something mid-morning or afternoon may well be taken as a significantly unfriendly sign: 'He was too mean even to offer a coffee!'

But a refreshment break can be used for more purposes than mere compliance with normal office courtesies. A pause for a cup of tea can be very helpful in lowering the emotional temperature if tempers have begun to rise. It can provide an opportunity for a quiet conversation between the two team leaders, or between the individual 'fixers' on each side. More deviously, the arrival of refreshments may - if the timing can be arranged unobtrusively - just happen to coincide with the other side's leader launching into a powerful peroration. There is nothing more deflating than the sudden rattle of cups as the door opens for the tea trolley. Delaying refreshments may also be an effective way of encouraging more rapid progress:

A negotiation between two company teams about a supply contract was getting badly bogged down in conflicting detail. 1 pm arrived with no conclusion having been reached on even the preliminary point of quantity discounts. The purchasing company's team leader then said: 'We've laid on a buffet lunch for 1.15 in the next room, but I think we ought to reach a decision on discounts before we break, otherwise we will all lose the threads of our arguments.' This ploy had been agreed within the company's team before the meeting started so they were quite relaxed about the delay, but by 2.15 the other firm's team were getting extremely restless and very eager to settle.

Documentation

Are minutes or other records of the meeting to be kept, if so, by whom and in what form? The point is an important one as it is not unknown for a verbal agreement to be reached within a negotiating meeting, only for the settlement to fall apart later when the two parties have a different understanding or recollection of what was said and of the details of the agreement.

The extreme in minute-keeping is the verbatim record, in which everything said in the negotiations is either tape-recorded or taken down by shorthand writers. It is a practice sometimes used in collective bargaining. It seems to have been introduced because neither party would accept the other's summary of what had been said, and because of disputes as to who had said what during very protracted negotiations. Apart from the cost and voluminous paperwork this method involved, it also back-fired on some of the participants when their casual comments were later put into cold print and circulated widely. One leading employer, for example, made an off-the-cuff comment at one meeting (intended humorously) that the annual conference of the National Union of Teachers reminded him of a chimpanzees' tea party. Set out in the formal minutes, this led to accusations by teachers that he thought they were no better than monkeys - not a helpful step in securing agreement to a very modest pay offer.

Normally, then, verbatim records cannot be recommended. The important thing about any effective negotiation is its outcome – the agreement - not the to and fro of argument which has led to this conclusion. There is, consequently, a good deal to be said for a written record which says little more than who was present, a brief summary of the opening positions of each side, and a full description of what was eventually agreed. This type of record does not require a formal minute taker. One of the team can be deputed to keep a note of the meeting, and if necessary clear this in draft with an opposite number in the other team before it becomes the formal record.

A fuller private record may be helpful, recording in complex negotiations the possibly different views or emphases of members of the other side, plus a note of points which emerged in discussion but which did not figure in the final agreement. But a private record of this kind should be kept as a background aid, not sprung on the other party as a secret weapon.

A good method of recording the outcome of informal, managerial negotiations, is for the manager taking the initiative in the discussion to confirm the outcome in a memo: 'Just a short note to confirm that we agreed yesterday to ... '

Key points

• Negotiations are influenced by their style and pace, by the composition of the negotiating team, and by the arrangements for seating, refreshments and documentation.
• Effective negotiators aim for a collaborative style but are prepared for confrontation.
• Other than in very informal negotiations, a team of three to five is advisable.
• Negotiations should be avoided while emotions are running high; but delay for its own sake is normally counterproductive.
• Inexperienced negotiators feel more confident on home ground, but for major, formal negotiations, the use of a neutral location may be desirable.
• Seating plans can be used to reinforce either a confrontational or a collaborative mode.
• Providing refreshments is not just a matter of common courtesy: refreshment breaks can be used to make progress in negotiations.
• Some record of the outcome of negotiations, however informal, is desirable in order to ensure a common understanding of what has been agreed.

Chapter 6 - Setting the Agenda

No negotiator can be effective unless the two parties have a common understanding of what it is they are discussing, why it is being discussed, and what each is seeking to achieve. This may seem obvious, yet misunderstandings about the content or purpose of negotiations are common causes of difficulty.

The personnel manager of an insurance company received a request from the local trade union branch for a meeting 'to discuss the unsatisfactory situation in the computer room.'
Because of previous complaints about ventilation, he assumed that this request also referred to environmental problems, and in preparation for the meeting he arranged for the building services engineer to carry out a series of checks on temperature and humidity. He then started the meeting by saying that he realized there had been problems in the past, but that recent checks had shown that a stable environment had now been achieved. It then transpired that the trade union wanted to talk about the layout of desks and VDUs, and their fears about a possible reorganization had been exacerbated by seeing the engineer in the room. The subsequent discussion was then adversely affected by the personnel manager having failed to prepare for the real issue, and by the trade union side being suspicious of the management's intentions.

It would clearly have been wise for the personnel manager to have clarified the subject matter of the meeting beforehand. It would also have been better for him to have invited the trade union to speak first when the meeting began.

There are two aspects to agenda-setting:

• Formally defining and agreeing with the other party what the discussion is about.

• Informally influencing the substance and character of the discussion.

The formal agenda

Even when negotiation is at its most informal, for example, two managers meeting to consider a matter of mutual interest – the effective manager establishes, whenever possible, what the subject matter is in advance.

Ed, the experienced, not to say wily, personnel manager referred to in the previous chapter, was well aware of this and would often try to obtain an advantage by initiating a meeting without explaining the real reason. For example, when he wanted to obtain the finance director's agreement to a budgetary change, he rang the director and said: 'May I drop in on you this afternoon? I want your advice on a small point.'
Until he spotted the ploy, the finance director used to agree, only to be confronted with an extremely well-prepared and skilfully presented case for something rather more than a minor concession. In response to such a request for a meeting, the director would now say: 'What's it about? I'm a bit pushed for time this afternoon so if you spend a couple of minutes on the phone now to fill me in, we can probably clear it more quickly when we meet.'

At the formal level, defining the subject matter of negotiations is often so important that it may itself be the subject of negotiation.

The media sometimes makes caustic comments about the time taken in national trade union disputes, or in international diplomacy, by 'talks about talks'. Although this may seem a time-wasting activity, it may be crucial for the success of the final negotiation. In an industrial relations pay dispute, for example, a subsidiary issue may arise about the dismissal of unofficial strikers. Both sides may want to make progress on the pay talks, but the trade union want to talk about the reinstatement of the dismissed employees as a pre-condition, while the employers are adamant that these dismissals are irreversible.

The only way of breaking the deadlock is to have discussions about what is to be discussed - and perhaps, how these discussions might be aided by the involvement of a third party.

In commercial negotiations, and in collective bargaining at company level, a simple exchange of correspondence is all that is needed. A meeting will be arranged, and the party initiating it will write to the other saying: 'This letter confirms the arrangement for us to meet (date, time, place) to discuss (subject) with a view to reaching agreement about (objective).' Any potential misunderstanding about the nature of the meeting can then be cleared up by telephone or further correspondence - the aim in all cases being to start the negotiations with a shared view of their purpose.

Influencing the agenda

The first main speaker in a negotiating session has some advantage in being able immediately to influence the tone of the meeting and the sequence or emphasis given to the various aspects of the subject under discussion. The party initiating the claim or request usually takes this advantage as it is logical for them to open the proceedings by stating their case. This does not mean that they should be allowed to introduce issues outside the already agreed agenda, but it does give them a scene-setting capability to influence the way the discussion will develop - the informal agenda.

It is, therefore, advantageous to claim this opening role if one wants to set the scene, rather than just respond. There is also a way of avoiding the simply reactive role, even when the other party must obviously be given the right of opening the formal negotiations. Ed's normal way of starting a negotiating session with his trade union officials illustrates this:

The union had submitted a claim for an increase in the overtime premium, and Ed had set up a meeting with them to discuss this. Conventionally, management would open such a meeting by turning to the trade union leader and saying: 'We are meeting to consider your claim for higher overtime payments, so perhaps you could begin by explaining your claim.'

This was not Ed's way. He liked to get in first. So his opening remark was: 'We are meeting to consider your overtime claim so we'll ask you to bat first. But before we start, it might be helpful if I just sketch in the background so that we are all in the same picture.' He then went on briefly to remind the union of the history of the current overtime arrangements and current overtime costs, dropping a hint that a joint study of unit costs might be a useful precursor to any change, and gently undermining the case he expected the union to have prepared. The phrase 'before we start' prevented an immediate union objection to management speaking first.

In managerial discussions, a similar technique can be used. The finance director faced with a well-prepared Ed making a bid for an improved budget could prevent Ed dictating the course of the meeting by making an early interruption: 'Before we go any further, I would find it helpful to remind ourselves of last year's discussions ...'

Despite initial efforts to define or influence the agenda, negotiations sometimes become bogged down in a confused discussion in which arguments become repetitive, or which lose sight of what each party is striving to achieve. This is particularly liable to occur when one party has a strong sense of grievance about the topic under discussion, and becomes more concerned with expressing these feelings than with working towards a solution; nor is it uncommon when dealing with inexperienced negotiators who have not fully prepared their case.

Three questions are useful in these circumstances to bring the negotiations into focus:

• 'We fully understand your views on this issue, but what are you actually asking us to do?'
• 'Are we right to think that the main point you want us to consider is x?'
• 'Is it clear that the main point we are making is y?'

Key points

• To be effective, the parties to negotiation need a common understanding of what is to be discussed and why.
• The subject, scope and purpose, therefore, need to be agreed before negotiations commence.

- For formal negotiations, this definition of the agenda should be in writing.
- The progress of a negotiation is influenced significantly by the first speaker.
- One way of securing this opening position is to volunteer a brief rehearsal of the background before full negotiations begin.
- Confused negotiations need re-focusing by a restatement of each party's key points.

Chapter 7 - Probing the Other Side's Case

Once negotiations are under way, three things need to be kept continually in mind:

• That the ultimate objective is to achieve an agreed outcome or solution, but that ...
• ... before making concessions, the other party's case should be rigorously probed or tested (and possibly weakened) and ...
• ... every reasonable opportunity should be taken to strengthen one's own position.

The first point lies behind every chapter of this book. This chapter looks at the second of these points - the need to test the validity of the other side's position. The next chapter deals with strengthening one's own case.

Exposing flaws

It is rare for one party to a negotiation to have a totally unanswerable case - though it is much less rare for a negotiator to *think* that this is so, and common for arguments to be presented as worthy of immediate acceptance. Flaws in a case may be intentional distortions, or may result from inadequate preparation or an unconscious assumption of being in the right. Negotiators are too often convinced by the force of their own arguments and consequently it is essential for the other party that these arguments are rigorously probed.
Particular points to look for are:

Errors of fact

No statement such as '10 per cent of deliveries have been two days late', or 'increases in clerical staff earnings have fallen behind the rise in the RPI', should be allowed to pass unchallenged. If these points are important to the negotiation, the party making such statements should be asked to produce the hard evidence to substantiate them.

Omissions of fact

It is very normal for a negotiator to build a case on correct but only partial, data. So 10 per cent of deliveries may well have been late, but the period under analysis included an unmentioned rail strike which distorted the statistics. Negotiators need to ask themselves and if necessary the other party - 'Is that the whole story? What other facts may be relevant?'
In a national negotiation about fire service pay, figures were given of the numbers of long service fire-fighters who had resigned during the previous six months. This was quoted as evidence that men were leaving the service because of low pay. What was omitted were' figures for the equivalent resignation rates over the previous five years. When these were produced it was evident that there had been no significant, recent change in the resignation rate.

Misuse of statistics

Perhaps the most common misuse of statistics is to quote averages for a very small number of cases, or to use averages to conceal a very wide range of actual data. 'The average time for a special production run last month was 28 hours against your contractual commitment of a 20 hour average.' But how many special production runs were there? There may have been too few for the average to be reliable.

Or the average may have been grossly distorted by just one case of 90 hours. Averages (or the arithmetic mean) should often be challenged by calling for details of the number of cases, the range of data, and the median and mode positions.

In a commercial negotiation about office rentals, one party claimed that average rents for equivalent premises in the locality had risen to £32 per sq foot. The other party was able to show that while this raw figure was accurate arithmetically, it concealed a range of £20 to £70, and that the median figure was only £27 – the average being distorted by just two unusually high rentals out of the 28 premises for which figures were available.

Faulty logic

Firm conclusions are often drawn from weak bases. 'Salaries are too low because staff are leaving for higher-paid jobs elsewhere' – but that is very normal: why should anyone leave for a lower salary, and unless one's own organization is the highest-paying in the industry, there will always be some firms paying more. Any key conclusion drawn by the other party needs to be examined closely against the basis on which it has been drawn.

Appeals to emotion

With a weak case in terms of fact or logic, it is normal for negotiators to fall back on emotional appeals. 'OK, so the company is short of cash and subject to fierce overseas competition - but it is still unfair that our members should be paid below the industrial average' or 'Wouldn't your company's reputation benefit from being seen to be generous, even though our client has no legal rights?' Concepts of fairness and reputation can be very powerful influences, and may well justify a case which is otherwise weak. It is not a matter of rejecting all such appeals. It is important, though, to recognize the basis of such arguments and consider them carefully and rationally before making concessions.

Testing the other side's case for flaws is best done by asking questions, rather than making counter-statements. Questions are less threatening but more revealing. It is much more effective, for example, even if the answer is known, to ask: 'On how many cases is your average figure based?', than to state: 'Your average figure is meaningless.' Apart from the direct questioning of facts (how many? how much? when?), more general, but useful probing questions, are:

• Could you explain your thinking about that more fully?
• We don't follow the logic of your argument: could you put it a different way?
• Isn't what you are really saying x? If so, how do you justify it?
• Could you explain the connection between x and y?

Testing credibility

It would be wrong to suggest that attempts should be made in *all* negotiations to undermine the credibility of the other side's leader. His or her standing with the team's members may justifiably be very high and, in that case, any attempt at belittlement would be counter-productive. The team will rally to their leader's support. There are occasions, however, when it may be judged that a vociferous and probably aggressive team leader does not have the unquestioned support of his or her team. In such cases, it is worthwhile trying to pin any flaws in the other party's case personally on the leader. If the team's confidence in their leader's credibility can be sapped, their ability to secure their original negotiating objectives will be markedly weakened. An industrial relations example illustrates this:

A trade union team was meeting with management to pursue a claim that an employee dismissed for a disciplinary offence should be reinstated. The trade union team consisted of a very aggressive and self-opinionated district official and five much less assertive shop stewards. All the talking was done by the district official who adopted an uncompromising stance, backed as he claimed, by case law arising from a recent decision of the Employment Appeals Tribunal. His team were obviously impressed by his apparent knowledge of the law, and the management allowed the argument in favour of reinstatement to be built very firmly on the legal position, although in reality the issue was one which was influenced almost entirely by local considerations.
The personnel manager then chose the moment to say: 'You would be right in your argument. George, except that you are out of date on your case law. Didn't you know that they overturned the Employment Appeals Tribunal decision last week? I've got the law report here if your team would like to see it.' The effect of course, was seriously to undermine the shop stewards' confidence in their district official's competence.

The innocent little question: 'Are you sure about that?' is a very powerful way of raising doubts about an opposing negotiator's credibility. It does no damage if they can substantiate what they have been saying, but saps both their own confidence and their standing in the eyes of their team if their argument is flawed.

Key points

• The other side's case should be tested for:

errors or omissions of fact
misuse of statistics
faulty logic
emotional appeal.

• The credibility of the other side's leader may need to be undermined, provided that this does not result in a defensive reaction.

Chapter 8 - Strengthening One's Own Case

The strength of one's own negotiating position depends partly on the power to make unilateral decisions (a point discussed in chapters 1 and 2), partly on the validity of the arguments one uses, and partly on the way these arguments are developed. This chapter is concerned with taking or making opportunities to strengthen one's position in the course of negotiating. There are two main aspects: identifying and reminding the other party of possible sanctions; and improving the impact of one's arguments and proposals by a variety of negotiating tactics.

Sanctions

Sanctions are concerned with power. They are the influences external to the details of the topic under discussion which may assist one party or the other to get its way. In the extreme, they are the means used to force a conclusion if negotiations fail.

So a commercial negotiation to settle a claim for the increased costs of a building contract, caused allegedly by the client's failure to provide an adequate specification, may be settled by an arbitrator or the courts if the two parties fail to agree between themselves. The party who think they have the best case may well use the threat of arbitration or court action as a negotiating sanction. Their negotiating tactics will include reminding the other party from time to time of the delays and costs involved if the claim is pursued through the courts, and that the probable outcome will favour the claimants.

In industrial relations, trade unions frequently use the threat of strike action as a sanction. 'Negotiate reasonably', is the message, 'or we'll walk out'. The employers' counter may be another form of sanction - the threat of a factory closure or job losses.

Constructive negotiation is not best conducted as an exchange of threats. People react against duress. But what is sometimes needed is the occasional reminder that there are certain realities about the situation, and that if all else fails, the use of a sanction may be inevitable.

So the negotiator's approach in a building contract case was: 'We would much prefer to reach an agreed conclusion but, if you persist in the line you are currently taking, we would have to think seriously about referring your claim to arbitration. Our legal advice is that while we would be ready to make some modest concessions - which we are still prepared to discuss- it is highly improbable that an arbitrator would give full support to your claim. Do you really want to have the delay and cost of an arbitration reference? Wouldn't it be better to try to make progress on an agreed basis?'

Chapters 13, 14, 15 and 19 take a more detailed look at the particular sanctions available in managerial, commercial and industrial relations negotiations. Here, the following checklist sets out the principal types of sanction which a negotiator can consider:
• Financial sanctions: increased costs resulting from stoppages or delays, changes to specifications, loss of business.
• Legal sanctions: the delays of the legal process; arbitration or compensation awards; injunctions to prevent action occurring; declarations of rights.
• Personal or organizational reputation: damage to the individual or company image caused by apparent intransigence, insensitivity, disregard of customer relations, or incompetence.
• Self regard: loss of 'face' resulting from failure to conclude a satisfactory agreement. (No real damage to the organization's or individual's formal or business interests may be involved, but the person's self-confidence and pride are hurt.)
• Emotional sanctions: appeals to a negotiator's sense of fairness or sympathy, regardless of the strict merits of a case.

Tactics

Three particular tactics may be used to strengthen a negotiator's position during the bargaining process:

- The introduction or exclusion of new issues
- Attaching conditions to concessions
- The use (and misuse) of emotion

The introduction of new issues

When discussing agenda-setting in chapter 6, the general principle was made that the subject and scope of a negotiation should be defined in advance. There are occasions, however, when the introduction of new issues may be advantageous. This is probably easier to achieve in an industrial relations context or between managers - situations in which both parties have an ongoing involvement in many matters other than the immediate point under discussion - than in a commercial setting. For example:

A personnel manager was meeting with the trade union, to consider the union's claim for a higher level of car allowances. She had agreed this as the subject for the negotiations and the claim was a simple one - that those staff who used their own cars at work, and whose cars were over 1 1/2 litres in engine size, should be paid at a higher rate than the existing allowance.
By agreeing to discuss the matter, the personnel manager had given an indication of some willingness to make a change - otherwise, she would have just said that the authority was not willing to make any alteration to the current allowance.

She decided to use the claim, however, to widen the discussion to include two new issues which the management wished to pursue. One was the use of leased cars for high business-mileage users (with a charge for private usage) as an alternative to car allowances. The other was the introduction of a more rigorous system of vetting expense claims.

By widening the scope of the negotiations, she was able to offset the costs of a small concession on car allowances by the agreed introduction of cost-saving measures on high mileage users and general expense payments.

This type of 'packaging' of issues - which may be possible to achieve only by introducing new elements once the negotiations are under way - offers more scope for compromise and trade-offs than the more intense bargaining involved in keeping strictly to single issues. Another use of new issues is to provide a diversion or breathing space if things are going badly. Another industrial relations case illustrates this:

The managing director of a publishing company was meeting the NUJ (the journalists' union branch) to consider a claim for increased annual leave. The union had prepared a much better case than the MD expected, and produced a great deal of evidence about other firms which showed how far theirs had fallen behind the rest of the industry.

Realizing that there could be no real argument about these comparisons, the MD stopped the discussion in its tracks by saying: 'Before we go any further, I have to say that this opens up the whole question of productivity. We really can't go on talking about more leisure time when what this company dearly needs is much more commitment to output while we are at work!'

This did not cause the union to withdraw their claim, but it prevented the MD being driven into a bargaining corner and gained him time to consider his position.

Of course, the other side may also use this tactic, and it is then a matter of judgment as to whether to accept the new point or firmly to reject it on the grounds that 'that isn't what we agreed this meeting would be about'. A related tactic which cannot be recommended, but which may be tried by a confrontational negotiator, is to use a personal attack as a diversion. The object is to throw the other party off balance - possibly by making them lose their temper - and so lose the thread of what was probably a strong argument.

In one inter-managerial discussion, John a sales manager was trying to persuade Stan, the production manager to change the production schedule. Stan was patiently resisting John's pressure, and embarked on an explanation of the whole production planning process and the high costs of an unplanned scheduling change. John went on the attack. 'That's your trouble, Stan, you're just a narrow-minded mechanic', he said fiercely.
'All you ever do is to defend the perfection of your damned computerized programme. When are you going to learn that there are real, live customers out there!'
If Stan was inexperienced, he might well have lost the thread of his argument at this by rising to the bait and defending his personal reputation. Instead, he used the effective negotiator's ploy of refusing to allow himself to be provoked, and deflected the attack with a good-humoured grin and a light-hearted comment about the honourable trade of the mechanic.

It may take much self-control not to react to a personal attack, but if one's negotiating strength is not to be weakened, such attacks need to be recognized for what they are - a mere diversionary ploy to be ignored or deflected unemotionally.

Attaching conditions to concessions

This is a key tactic in effective negotiation. Compromise and concession are of course, essential aspects of negotiation - otherwise no bargaining can occur - but every effort should be taken to minimize the loss of benefit involved. This is partly just a matter of hard bargaining against the background of the two parties' relative power. Against a union claim for a 9 per cent wage increase, 6Y:z per cent may be a reasonable settlement if the union's case and its ability to apply sanctions is weak: 8 per cent may be a good settlement if the reverse is true. But another approach is to introduce a condition to the settlement - something for something rather than something for nothing.

How is this best done? The golden rules are:

• Introduce the condition before talking about the concession.
• Do not give details of the concession until there is an indication that the condition is negotiable.

If the possibility of a concession is raised before the condition, the other party will seize on it as an offer and it will then be difficult to say that it is conditional. To give details of what the concession might be before the other side have shown any willingness to consider the condition, runs similar risks. Two industrial relations cases illustrate the point:

A trade union had submitted a claim for a shorter working week and longer annual leave. The company was ready to make some movement on total working time but did not want to alter current patterns of shift work, so the management response, put briefly, was: 'If you are prepared to set aside this year's claim far a shorter working week, we might be able to talk about annual leave.' The condition - dropping the working week claim - was put first, so any concession would clearly be conditional. No details of the possible concession were given, pending an indication by the union that they were prepared to consider the condition.

A union was claiming a 10 per cent wage rise, the management had offered 7 1/2 per cent but were under great pressure to go further. The line they then took was: 'If we were to consider going any higher we would have to bring forward a proposal we had originally intended to put to you later in the year - the need to introduce a Saturday shift on plain time instead of overtime rates.' So any concession on wages (unspecified at this stage) would clearly be conditional on agreement about a wholly new issue.

The use of emotion

A general rule in negotiating is to avoid becoming emotionally committed. It is difficult to exercise the necessary imagination and flexibility if one has developed a strong, personal or emotional commitment to a fixed point of view. As already noted, it is also dangerous to rise to the bait of a personal attack. It is the issues which should be concentrated on, not the defence of personal dignity or the scoring of debating points.

There are occasions, however, when a controlled display of emotion may be beneficial. The two conditions are that the emotion *must* be sincere, and its use should be a *conscious* decision, not an instant reaction. Two examples follow:

A negotiation about a supply contract between the managerial teams of two firms had degenerated into little better than a slanging match on points of detail. This was brought to an end by one older manager, much respected in the industry, interrupting the argument with an obviously deeply-felt plea that all concerned should set personal differences aside, respect each other's professional competence, and concentrate on finding a solution to the business problem involved.

A trade union leader swayed the employers' attitudes in a wage bargaining session by a very sincere and strongly felt plea that some improvement should be made to wage rates for the lowest paid categories - mainly women working part-time in cleaning and catering. He admitted that in strict market or supply and demand terms, his case was weak. But by quoting actual cases of real hardship, and appealing to the employers' sense of fairness and human sympathy, he created an emotional mood in which the employers found it very difficult to do other than respond favourably.

Key points

• One's own negotiating position can be strengthened by identifying and tactfully reminding the other party of sanctions which are available if negotiations fail.
• Sanctions may be financial, legal or emotional, or may relate to the effect of a particular outcome on an organization's or individual's reputation, image or self-regard.
• New issues may be introduced into a negotiation as a diversion, or to provide opportunities for trade-offs between parts of a bargaining package.
• Whenever possible, conditions should be attached to concessions - something for something rather than something for nothing.

• When considering concessions, introduce the condition first and do not give details of the concessions until the other party shows some willingness to negotiate on the condition.

• Normally, avoid emotional commitment, but displays of emotion may occasionally be beneficial provided that they are sincere and used consciously.

Chapter 9 - Timing and Adjournments

People with no negotiating experience sometimes express surprise at how long negotiations can take. 'What on earth can they be talking about all that time?' is a comment often made about nationally publicized negotiations, or a long series of lengthy meetings to resolve an industrial dispute. There are several reasons for this tendency to go on talking rather than moving briskly towards an agreement – and the trend is one that applies to all negotiations, however informal.

• Unlike a formal business meeting with a detailed agenda and an average of perhaps ten minutes for each separate item, negotiations often involve a joint exploration of the subject matter and a careful sounding out of alternatives and possible compromise. The two sides start from different viewpoints and need time to test and explain their differing perceptions and objectives. In search for a mutually satisfactory solution, each is cautious about conceding too much, too quickly. It is not possible to handle this process of probing, floating ideas and compromise on a very structured basis: the process is organic rather than mechanistic- and that takes time.

• That said, there is sometimes a tendency to assume that the negotiations will be lengthy and, therefore, to set neither a time-scale nor a target completion time or date.

• Knowing that concessions will have to be made, some negotiators are concerned to demonstrate that these are not made lightly. An agreement which is concluded in half an hour may, they feel, give an impression that they have not fought hard enough for their side's objectives. Only after a very lengthy period of hard argument and bargaining do they feel able to modify their opening position. This is particularly the case when the negotiating team has to report back to their principals - the board of directors, say, for a management team or a mass meeting of union members for the trade union officials.

Despite these trends, there are some aspects of timing which have a major impact on the effectiveness of negotiations, and the effective negotiator will continuously be aware of the changes of mood and attention which the passage of time can bring. The two main points to consider are the duration of each negotiating session and the use of adjournments.

The duration of sessions

When planning a negotiation, some thought should be given to the time-scale and an attempt made to strike a balance between an open-ended arrangement - which encourages unduly lengthy talks - and providing too little time for a constructive discussion. The party taking the initiative in calling the meeting has an advantage here. They can suggest how much time to set aside, or announce when the meeting starts that, for example, 'We have another appointment later this morning, so we need to aim to finish by 11am'. If it is obvious from the start that the matter is complex and will require more than one meeting, dates and times can be set aside at the opening session. There is no doubt that having a target finishing time - provided that it is realistic - does help to create a positive attitude and a feeling that progress towards a conclusion is being made.

There is evidence, too, that the maximum time it is possible to maintain a high degree of continuous attention and positive involvement is little over two hours. Two hours is a reasonable period to set aside for a single, relatively straightforward negotiation; or to spend in one uninterrupted session during a longer bargaining episode.

There is a time factor, too, in the presentation of cases and arguments. If it is thought necessary to open proceedings by making a prepared presentation - as might be the case with a catering contractor's team bidding to secure a service contract - 15 to 20 minutes is probably the longest period to ensure the other party's full interest and attention; and this period should be announced by the presenter: 'We'd like to start by telling you about our service, and we've prepared a 15 minute presentation which we hope you will find interesting.' This prior statement about the time helps to prevent the other party's attention wandering, and reassures them that they will not have to sit through an interminable talk.

At the more informal level , the longest period one person is likely to hold attention during the to and fro of a discussion is as short as two to three minutes. To go beyond that, runs the risk of irritating the other side by appearing to want to dominate the discussion or to
prevent them from responding effectively. In summary:

• The longest period for effective continuous negotiation is about two hours.
• The optimum time for a prepared presentation is 15 to 20 minutes.
• The longest time for an individual contribution to a discussion is two to three minutes.

The fact that major set-piece negotiations often do not accord with these guidelines is more a matter of logistics than tactics. Top level negotiators with extremely full diaries assemble from all over the country on a fixed date, many with equally important appointments on the following day. There is then a mutual desire to complete the business on the appointed day to avoid disrupting the next day's arrangements. When negotiating difficulties then arise, the only solution is to go on bargaining into the night hours - well past the point at which it is possible for most people to maintain an alert and balanced approach. Bargaining to exhaustion has its place in the annals of negotiation but cannot be recommended as a normal or effective tactic.

Adjournments

It follows from the two-hour rule, that in a bargaining session which needs to run for a longer period, breaks or adjournments should be taken at around the two hour mark. Normally, these can be timed to coincide with a refreshment break.

Adjournments may, though, be suggested at any time and there are at least three other constructive uses of the *ad hoc* (as distinct from scheduled) break:

• To give the parties an opportunity to withdraw and review progress among themselves or consider a proposal put by the other side. There is no need to respond immediately or intuitively to a proposition from the other side. Just say: 'That's an interesting new point which we need time to consider. I suggest we break for 20 minutes so that my side can talk it over among ourselves.'
• To provide a break if the negotiations have reached an impasse or have become bogged down in trivia or personal argument. Again, it is just a matter of taking the initiative in suggesting: 'I think it might be helpful if we had a short break at this point so that we can each consider where the discussion is going.' It is surprising how much the atmosphere of a negotiation can improve after a short interruption of this kind.
• To provide an opportunity for one or two members of each side to talk informally with each other away from the bargaining table.

It may be possible to explore ways forward in a very informal manner which would not be appropriate in the formal bargaining arena. So the leader of one side, sensing that the moment is right for such a suggestion, might say to his or her opposite number: 'Do you agree that it might be helpful if we adjourn for half an hour while you and I consider, without formal commitment, whether progress might be made by a different approach?' It is not possible, of course, to insist on such an arrangement - but the negotiator on the other side may well agree that it is worth trying. The comment about 'no commitment' is made to reassure the others in the two teams that their leaders will not strike any formal deal without prior reference back.
The effective use of adjournments of the three kinds just outlined is

a very important skill to acquire. Any experienced negotiator can quote numerous examples of negotiations which succeeded primarily because adjournments were used to stop unconstructive argument or to open the door to informal soundings between leaders from which eventual solutions have emerged.

Inexperienced negotiators should also pay particular attention to the value of an adjournment to create time to consider unexpected developments. There is never an excuse for being 'bounced' into an unsatisfactory agreement. One party cannot prevent the other from taking time out to review their position, and if such time is needed, an adjournment is the way to secure it.

Key points

• In planning and conducting negotiations, positive attention should be paid to the duration of bargaining sessions, formal presentations and individual contributions to the discussion.
• A continuous session should rarely exceed two hours, a formal presentation 15 to 20 minutes, and an informal contribution two to three minutes .
• Adjournments coincident with refreshments should be used to break a lengthy negotiation into two-hour segments.
• Adjournments should be used as powerful aids to negotiation by:
- providing time to consider progress or new proposals within the team, and avoiding snap decisions
- bringing unconstructive or personalized arguments to an end
- providing an opportunity for informal, exploratory talks between individual members of the two parties.

Chapter 10 - Searching for Common Ground

Inexperienced negotiators tend to over-concentrate on the adversarial aspects of negotiation - defending their own opening positions and trying to expose flaws in the other party's case. There is a role for these aspects, particularly if the other party adopts an aggressive stance, but they should not dominate or set the tone of the negotiations if this can be avoided. It should always be kept in mind that the purpose of a negotiation is *to reach an agreement,* not to demonstrate one's own virtues or to score points off the opposition.

An agreement, by definition is an outcome in which both parties come together and see some advantage. Negotiating towards agreement means moving from different positions towards common ground.

This constructive approach is particularly, though by no means exclusively, relevant to negotiation between managers. Underlying the substance of daily managerial relationships within any organization there is - or should be - a common concern for the well-being of the organization as a whole. Managers often become involved in heated arguments about the merits of conflicting ideas or proposals.

Too often, defending one's own view (in reality, defending personal pride or prestige) can become the objective of the argument. The wise manager will depersonalize such arguments by standing back from the disputed detail and encouraging those involved to examine the issue from a corporate organizational viewpoint. Which of the disputed ideas will best serve the interests of the company? Which best fits the organization's values or style?

As well as a general emphasis on the need to search for common ground, this chapter looks at several ways of reducing tension and disagreement and identifying the shared interests on which an agreement may eventually be constructed:

- Listening and asking questions
- The use of humour
- Reading between the lines -looking for 'coded' signals
- Looking for links between the two cases.

Listening

One of the most common negotiating faults is saying too much and listening too little. Of course, in the opening phase of a negotiation it is necessary to state one's position and make an initial response to the case made by the other party. But once both parties' positions are clear, the discussion needs to move into a more collaborative or exploratory phase in which the search is on for common ground and a mutually acceptable outcome. In this phase, acute attention needs to be given to what the other side are saying and how they say it.

What are their real concerns? How might they react to a possible way forward? Are they beginning to shift their ground? The answers will be found by perceptive listening, not by continuing to talk.

It may be thought that if the other party also adopts a listening posture, the discussion will dry up. To prevent this, the tactic is to switch from making statements or rebutting arguments to asking questions - and listening intently to the tone, as well as the substance, of the answers.

Aileen Kenney was the marketing manager of a low-cost furniture manufacturer. The production director was John Steel. a no-nonsense, efficiency-minded manager with little time for the niceties of public relations. There had recently been some very adverse publicity about the fire risks of the company's products in the local press, following two child deaths in a house fire. The regional television station had just telephoned John, asking for him to be interviewed on the subject. He had refused, telling the reporter he had nothing to say, but that they might contact the marketing manager. He told Aileen he had said this. She went to see him to discuss what the company response should be.

Initially, the discussion was extremely sticky. 'Tell them what you like', said John. 'Provided that you don't commit me to doing anything.' Aileen was very unhappy with this. She pointed out that this put her in an impossible position if she was to project the company in a favourable light. She wanted to say that there was a current problem with the availability of flame-proofed materials, but that the company, while in no different position from most others in the industry, had plans well in hand for new, improved product ranges. She argued, too, that the story was likely to be given to the national press if the company upset the local media. 'That's not my worry', was John's reply.

Aileen then switched to a questioning approach. 'Forget the present case for the moment', she suggested: 'What is the general trend in the use of new materials in the industry over the next five years?' John began to talk technicalities, which she encouraged. 'How many weeks' stock have we got of the old materials?' she asked. 'Are there significant production problems in a phased introduction of the new materials?' She went on: 'If I felt we could live with a price increase of 5 per cent, would that cover any increased material costs?'

By the questioning process, it eventually became apparent that John's intransigence about the television interview was not based on a cool, analytical assessment of the situation, looked at from a company viewpoint, but a resentful reaction to what he had felt was implied personal criticism. By drawing this out, and then asking John for interesting information about new production plans, she was able to agree a very positive line to take in the television interview. Questions, rather than statements were the key to her success, linked to an emphasis on what was good for the company.

The use of humour

Negotiations are serious matters, and there is no place for flippancy. Humour, and the occasional light-hearted remark can be used, however, to relieve tension and contribute to establishing a shared, rather than confrontational, relationship.

It is interesting to observe the first few minutes' interaction between two experienced negotiators - either as individuals or teams. Almost inevitably, there is a short period of good-natured banter. 'Open the windows,' the leader of one party will say, 'George has brought his fumigator!' - referring to the other leader's pipe. To which George will respond: 'I brought it to kill the bugs in your office!' Why is this sort of ritual both normal and useful? It serves two functions: helping to reduce the underlying tension, and encouraging a joint, rather than confrontational, mode.

This bonding is not particularly strong. It can easily break down under the later pressure of serious disagreement. But most negotiations make better progress if the initial ritual *bonhomie* is reinforced from time to time during the discussions by a well-timed, light hearted or humorous comment. This is not a matter of interrupting the discussion to tell irrelevant jokes, nor does it call for any great wit. Indeed, the too-clever remark may be seen as sarcasm rather than humour. It usually involves spotting the occasional absurdity or mistake (if possible in what one's own side have said) and drawing attention to its funny side. Its implication must be that we are all in this together, we're all human and fallible, and let's all keep a sense of proportion. It is, unfortunately, impossible to define in terms of a formula or set of principles - but it should not be overlooked.

Reading between the lines

Experienced negotiators are very wary of committing themselves to definite statements until they are confident that this will not prejudice their position. Their initial moves will be hedged about with reservations, or couched in indeterminate form so that they can quickly withdraw before the other party can seize on a statement as a specific concession. When the negotiation is in its exploratory phase it is, consequently, of great importance that every hint of a change of position or a possible way forward is picked up.

There is a whole vocabulary of such 'coded' messages or signals. A few of the more common, together with their interpretations, are:

• 'There is no possibility of our going that far at this stage.' *But there may be a possibility of movement later.*

- 'It would not be our normal business practice to do that.' *But if the price was right, we might make an exception.*
- 'You have put these proposals in a form which we find unacceptable.' *But if they were repackaged, some progress might be possible.*
- 'What we must make clear is that points (a) and (b) are totally unacceptable.' *But points (c) and (d) are worth talking about.*
- 'We can certainly agree on the basic principles.' *But there are still major problems with the actual details.*

Hints and signals are not always verbal. They may be identified from changes in tone, facial expression or posture. A note of hesitation or embarrassment may creep in if the speaker has no conviction in what is being said. A combative pose - arms folded or hands clenched - may be changed to a more open or relaxed position. There may be a change of spokesperson within the team, with an assertive speaker making way for someone who has been quietly listening up to this point.

Understanding and looking for the signals carried by body language can help the effective negotiator interpret the real meanings which may be hidden behind the actual words being used.

Looking for links

Both parties to a negotiation share at least two objectives. One is the general wish, whatever the subject, to reach a satisfactory outcome, preferably without unpleasantness or over-lengthy time involvement. The other, specific to each case, is that the agreement should have some benefit or advantage.

The first can be used to encourage the other party to co-operate in maintaining a reasonably brisk, business-like pace and equable atmosphere to the negotiation. If the discussion becomes bogged down in trivia, repetition or personal acrimony, an appeal can be made to the parties' joint interest in making progress and avoiding time-wasting. As the leader in one negotiation put it: 'I am sure neither side wants to spend their valuable time picking over the bones - wouldn't it be better if we set aside our current argument and concentrated on the main point at issue.'

The second point - that the parties share an interest in a favourable outcome - may not be quite so obvious. Each side's interpretation of 'favourable' will be different. Yet ultimately they will have to take joint responsibility for an agreement - and each needs to be able to consider this to be at least acceptable before they can be expected to endorse it. The link between them is the common action or outcome which they do eventually agree, and their joint need to consider this outcome justified.

The advantage may, of course, be somewhat one-sided. An employer may agree a high wage settlement fairly grudgingly, with all the perceived advantage going to the trade union. Yet even here, there are links between the parties which will help the employer come to terms with the outcome. Directly, the settlement will remove the sanction of industrial action. More constructively, it will help the employer achieve or improve his recruitment and retention capability.

In working towards an agreement, it is, consequently, helpful to consider not just the pros and cons of alternative outcomes to one's own side, but to think also of what common interest exists, and what benefits each alternative has for the other side.

In a factory dispute, the trade union was demanding the dismissal of a foreman for alleged racial abuse towards a black employee. The company felt it had to resist this because it was the first time any complaint of this kind had been made against the foreman, and because he was in all other respects one of their most experienced and competent supervisors. So the opening positions of the two sides were diametrically opposed - dismissal or no dismissal.

The eventual agreed solution was a warning to the foreman, an apology to the employee and the introduction of an equal opportunity training programme for all supervisory staff. The link between the two sides which led to this outcome was that both were concerned to ensure that no such incident occurred again. The training programme was seen by both parties as being a far more constructive way of achieving this than the dismissal which the union had originally sought.

A concentration on common interests, instead of on the original differences, is a key to effective negotiation. If the possible solution to an apparently narrow and hotly-disputed issue can be shown to contribute to the achievement of broader objectives, breaking a deadlock and reaching agreement is often made easier. These common interests often include:

• Company success and business prosperity
• Job security
• Company reputation - both commercially and as a good employer
• Avoidance of wastage or environmental damage
• Individual reputation - for professionalism, integrity, skill
• An image of being constructive as a negotiator
• Maintenance of high morale
• Avoiding interference by third parties.

Key points

• The purpose of a negotiation is to reach agreement, not to score points in argument.
• Effective negotiators are good listeners: they ask questions more than they make statements.
• Humour, or good-natured banter, can be used to reduce tension and help create a bond between the parties.
• It is important to look for verbal and non-verbal clues or signals of the other party's changes of mood or approach.
• There should be a concentration on issues or outcomes of common interest, rather than on the original differences.

Chapter 11 - Working Towards Agreement

There comes a point in all negotiations when the discussion needs to move from an exploration of the issues, and a careful sounding out by each party of the other's possibly changing position, to a positive consideration of specific proposals for agreement. Handling this phase well is crucial. One bad or tactless move and the other side's willingness to reach agreement may be lost. Several aspects of this phase need to be considered:

- The use of periodic summaries
- Using hypothetical suggestions
- Helping the other party to move
- A voiding loss of face
- Constructive compromise.

Periodic summaries

In a negotiation in which a number of issues are involved, it is not unusual for progress to be made faster on some matters than others.
Unless this is defined and accepted as it occurs, there is a danger that a later disagreement on another issue may lead to back-tracking and the loss of earlier progress.
It is helpful, therefore, to pause from time to time to summarize where the discussion has led and thus secure a step-by-step movement towards eventual full agreement. The negotiation about working time, quoted in several previous examples, can be used to illustrate this:

The discussion had reached the point at which it had become clear that levels of overtime were a key issue which now needed discussion. At this point, the management side's leader said: 'Before we go on to talk about overtime, I think we might all find it helpful to summarize where we have got to so far. The company has explained why it cannot consider a reduction in the working week. But we have accepted that some movement should be made on annual leave, and our proposition - which I take it you have agreed, at least in principle - is that the manual employees' entitlement should be harmonized with that of the clerical staff. Is everyone happy with that summary? If so, we'll just make a quick note of it so that we don't waste time later trying to remember what we said.' The effect of this summary was to lock both parties in to an agreed approach to the annual leave issue, and prevent a possible dispute on overtime upsetting the progress which had already been made.

A summary may, of course, reveal that the two sides have different understandings about the position which has been reached. This may be frustrating - but it provides a useful opportunity to clear up any differences during the negotiation. However, it is even more frustrating when it seems that a final agreement has been reached, only to discover differences of understanding about a point both parties have assumed to have been settled earlier.

Hypothetical suggestions

The introduction of specific proposals after a period of cautious exploration of the issues is sometimes a difficult transition to handle. One way of easing into it is initially to float the proposals as hypothetical or on a no-commitment basis. This enables the other party to present their initial reactions as similarly provisional, and one's own side to withdraw without losing their bargaining flexibility.

Jenny Sadler. a local authority finance manager, was trying to persuade Ronald Gower, the housing manager, to accept a new method of costing maintenance work. He was wedded to his present system which was proving difficult to computerize and while giving him the information he needed for day to day purposes, involved too much manual processing time in the finance department. At an earlier meeting, Jenny had presented him with a fully worked out and completely changed system which he had rejected out of hand as being designed solely to help the accountants. This time she changed her tactics.

'Looking at it from your point of view: she said, 'What might your reaction be if it was possible to simplify the daily work sheets which your supervisors have to complete? I'm not sure how far we could take this, but if you are willing to consider it, without commitment at this stage, I could work up something specific.' George agreed that this was worth taking further, and Jenny was able to go on to another element in her plan, selling this on a similar basis of the benefits in it to George, and the absence of pressure on him to give an immediate, final Yes or No.

Floating ideas in this way gets proposals onto the table without creating a strong commitment by one party to defend them, or the other to oppose. A more relaxed discussion can ensue, with adjustments to the original idea arising jointly, rather than being perceived as victories or defeats. Some typical phrases used in introducing proposals in this way are:

• 'Just for the sake of argument, what might your views be if we suggested that ... '
• 'Without pressing you for a formal response, what would your feeling be about ... ?'
• Suppose we thought of doing something along these lines – how might you react?'
• 'We had thought that we might suggest x, but we are not sure that this is quite what you had in mind.'

• Have you thought about y? It is something we might find possible to consider.'

Helping the other party to move

Two very human tendencies can inhibit progress in the closing stages of negotiation:

• A reluctance to be seen to be modifying one's original position.
• A temptation to gloat over any retreat by the other party.

These tendencies are exacerbated by viewing negotiation in terms of winning and losing, rather than as a process of reaching a jointly satisfactory outcome. One of the most important ways of achieving such an outcome is to make it as easy as possible for the other side to shift their position and agree to compromise - rather than making them feel that they are on the losing side.

This may mean going beyond the search for common ground, discussed in chapter 10, and emphasizing the particular and different benefits which a proposed outcome offers to the other party. Consider the case of a company negotiating with its trade unions about the introduction of a cashless pay system.

The company's objective was primarily to introduce a much less costly system of wage payments - in effect, to save money on pay administration. Their real case was that the current cash payment system was out-dated and expensive. But to expect the trade union to agree to a change simply to help the company financially was unrealistic. To help the trade union move towards acceptance of a change, the company needed to identify and explain the benefits to union members. These were described in terms of the advantages of operating bank accounts (a deal had been done with a local bank branch to offer incentives for employees opening accounts) and the elimination of the risk of employees becoming injured in a wages raid.

The company's aim was to provide the union officials with a case which could be sold to union members as advantageous to them.

Another tactic is to respond positively rather than critically to any advance, however small, offered by the other side. If, after hours of tedious argument, the other side suggest a minor concession, the temptation may be to reply: 'We could have saved a lot of time if you had agreed to that in the first place instead of wasting two hours defending the indefensible!' Better by far to bite one's tongue and say instead: 'That's a very interesting and responsible suggestion. I am sure it provides a basis for making some real progress.'

Helping the other party to move involves:

• Helping them to identify the benefits to their side.
• Playing down the benefits to one's own side.
• Encouraging every positive move they make, however small.
• Applauding the other party's wisdom and helpfulness in making positive movement.
• Avoiding any implication that by moving, they are losing and one's own party is winning.

Saving face

Lying behind much of the reluctance to accept a compromise is loss of face - the fear of apparent personal failure, openly exposed. It is as important to recognize this as a potentially inhibiting factor in oneself as it is to avoid acting in a way which exacerbates the fear in the other party.

Fear of loss of face can be an inhibiting factor in two ways. It may prevent good ideas emerging within one's own team: it may also work against the making of constructive proposals to or from the other party.

A management team was negotiating an office rent review with a team from the property company who owned their HQ building. The first meeting ended in deadlock and a further meeting had to be scheduled. The management leader called a pre-meeting of his own side for a post-mortem on what had happened and to plan for the next negotiation. One of his team members then said that he had thought that an offer to consider a full repairing lease (under the current lease, the property company were responsible for repairs) might have broken the deadlock. 'Why didn't you suggest that at the time 7' asked the management leader. The reply was: 'I didn't want to be the first one to make a concession.'

The person involved had been more concerned with his reputation within his own team as a tough negotiator than with making progress in the negotiations. The ironic feature of these negotiations was that when the two teams next met, the property company started by suggesting that a lower rental might be acceptable if a full repairing lease was introduced - and a mutually satisfactory deal was soon concluded.

Asked informally sometime later why the property firm had not suggested this solution at the first meeting, their leader said: 'We didn't want to be the first to make a concession.'

Personal and corporate pride (which is the basis of 'face') had prevented progress both within and between the teams in this example. There is a related point. Loss of face can occur when either party gets itself boxed into a position from which the only escape appears to be a humiliating retreat. An example might be an unequivocal statement that 'this is our absolutely final offer and under no circumstances can we make any further concessions' – only to be confronted with a further and unexpected argument (or demonstration of strength) by the other party which can only be dealt with by a further compromise. The danger is that instead of accepting the humiliation of having to admit that the final offer is not final, negotiations will be broken off and resort will be had to a more confrontational method of proceeding.

Three things follow from this:

• Unless one is very sure of one's position, do not adopt a stance from which movement will be perceived as defeat: always leave a back-door open for a more dignified withdrawal.
• But at the same time, do not be thin-skinned about the comment which the other party may make about changes of position. Do not allow considerations of face to get in the way of sensible compromise.
• If necessary, help the other party to keep their back door open, so that they are not provoked into aggression or confrontation by feeling trapped.

Constructive compromise

There is more than window-dressing or manipulation in seeking to show that a proposed solution has advantages to both parties. The achievement of genuinely constructive compromise involves the widest possible view being taken of what beneficial elements can be included in the agreement. It also involves consideration of wider issues, such as the effect of the negotiations on the quality of the longer-term relationship between the two parties. For example, a company will not want to damage an otherwise excellent commercial relationship with a key supplier by a dispute over a short-term delivery problem: and in industrial relations, it has always to be remembered that company and trade union have to continue their coexistence after each negotiation.

Compromise is often thought of as negative. But to avoid costly confrontation and to secure an effective agreement in which both parties can share a sense of satisfaction and achievement, compromise is both positive and constructive. So in moving towards the conclusion of a negotiation, thought needs to be given to how the advantages in the final agreement can be optimized. Questions which assist this process are:

• Can this or that proposal be used to achieve a wider benefit than first seems possible?
• Can a new condition be introduced to offset the disadvantages of a pending concession?
• Would a change of emphasis or priority secure long-term advantage against short-term loss?
• Might a tactical retreat on a narrow issue now, provide a better basis for beginning negotiations on another issue later?
• Can agreement on an apparently minor issue create a useful precedent for use at some later stage?
• Can the negotiation and its outcome be used to create or improve a favourable, more general, relationship with the other party?

It is on questions of this kind that thought needs to be concentrated, rather than worrying about the possibility of every minor compromise being perceived as weakness.

Key points

• The closer a negotiation is to reaching agreement, the more sensitively the discussion needs to be handled.
• Periodic, jointly agreed summaries of progress can secure a phased agreement and prevent reversion to earlier argument.
• Proposals may initially be put as hypothetical suggestions. This makes it easier for both parties to avoid the pressure of immediate acceptance or withdrawal.
• There is a positive advantage in making it easy for the other side to move, rather than challenging them on a win/lose basis.
• Proposals are best sold on their advantages to the other party, not to one's own.
• Fear of losing personal or corporate face can severely inhibit progress.
• Compromise should be seen as constructive, not weakness.
• In assessing the benefits of an agreement, consideration should be given to factors beyond the context of the immediate negotiation - such as the creation of useful precedents, and the quality of long-term relationships.

Chapter 12 - Clinching Agreement

The final stage in any successful negotiation is the conclusion of an agreement. Even in very informal managerial discussions, an agreed outcome is sought, otherwise there has been no more than a non-productive exchange of views. At the other extreme, in formal commercial bargaining, the outcome is an agreement which will carry legal weight as an enforceable contract. Securing an effective agreement is aided by paying attention to four aspects:

- Closing the deal- timing and credibility
- Ensuring all points have been included
- Ensuring full understanding - summaries and documentation
- Avoiding fudging the issues merely to secure an agreement.

Closing the deal

It is critical in a negotiation to judge when the time has come to bring the exploratory and concession-making stages to an end, to indicate that one can go no further, and to suggest that an agreement be concluded on the basis of the positions which have been reached by that time. Two factors are important: timing, and the credibility of the final position.

It is in the nature of negotiation that the mood or emotional atmosphere of a meeting fluctuates between highs and lows. At one point, things will be going well with a feeling of co-operation and *bonhomie;* then the mood changes as a serious disagreement arises. It is fairly obvious that the right time to bring the negotiation to a successful conclusion is during a high - or at least not during, or in the immediate aftermath, of a bad patch. An adjournment can be used to close the door on an unsatisfactory episode, and enable a fresh start to be made - perhaps of the final session.

What is sometimes less easy is to convince the other party that no further concessions or compromise are possible; that one has reached the end of the road and that decisions must now be reached as to whether to settle or close the negotiation without agreement.

This is particularly difficult if you have made a series of minor concessions or revised offers during a lengthy bargaining process, and have unwisely described an earlier position as being 'the last offer'. The other party will have learned from this that your 'last' may not mean final- how are they to know that you have, in reality, reached your sticking point?

Statements about finality can, however, be reinforced in several ways:

• Tone of voice and choice of words: a clear, firm, confidently expressed, unapologetic statement that: 'We've moved quite a way during this meeting and have taken full account of everything you have put to us. We are now at the point where you must decide whether or not to accept what we have just proposed. It's our absolute limit.'
• Change of style: from a discursive mode to a short, crisp statement.
• Non-verbal behaviour: such as gathering up all one's papers and putting them in a document case.
• Change of format: from purely verbal proposals to the tabling of a written final offer - even if this is no more than a quickly handwritten note, passed across the table.

Even when the timing is right and the credibility of the final offer has been established, it may still be necessary to add something to tip the balance in favour of an acceptance. Among the aids to breaking any last-minute deadlock are:

- Tying the agreement to some future benefit: 'If we can settle on the terms we have just proposed, we would be willing to re-open discussions on x not later than the end of next year.'
- Agreeing that a disputed point can be subject to review: 'We understand why you are reluctant to accept x, and we would be willing to include a review of its effect in 12 months time.'
- Explaining fully why no further concessions are possible, perhaps by bringing in a new member of the management team to add weight to the case. (For example, the sales director might be asked to join the meeting to explain the difficult trends in the overseas market.)
- Pointing out the adverse consequences of a failure to reach agreement - not in a threatening way but as a cold recitation of fact: 'Much as we wish to avoid it, a failure to agree at this stage would force us to consider legal action - and our lawyers tell us that we should then plan for a 12 month delay and costs on both sides running at over £50,000.'

Ensuring all points have been included

In the euphoria of reaching agreement on a major issue - a wage award, say, or a price for a new contract - it is not unknown for some subsidiary but still important points to be left unclarified.

A daily newspaper negotiated an agreement with the owners of a car racing circuit for the newspaper's name to be emblazoned permanently across a bridge spanning the track.
The site ensured that TV cameras frequently panned across the bridge during televized races. Some years later, the circuit owners decided that for safety reasons, the bridge had to be re-sited. Unfortunately for the newspaper, the new site was not in the TV cameras' line of sight.

The newspaper claimed that the agreement implied a right to have their name displayed at the original bridge site. The circuit owners disagreed, and the matter had, eventually, to be resolved in the high court (in favour of the circuit owners).

This expensive dispute could have been avoided if thought had been given in the original negotiations to the need to define what would happen if the bridge had ever to be removed.

Failures to define dates - of implementation, review, or duration are among the most common omissions. Other faults include a failure to define terms (e.g. does 'wage' mean basic rate, or basic rate plus allowances; does 'normal working week' include routine overtime?).

Ensuring full understanding

The last point related closely to the need to ensure, not just that everything necessary has been included in the agreement, but that the two parties have a common understanding of its terms and intentions. Verbally, it is important for the person taking the lead in the negotiation to make a final summary: 'I think we have now reached agreement on all the issues. My understanding is that what we have agreed to is ... ' going on to list each point.

Assuming there is verbal agreement with this summary, the sooner it is committed to writing the better. In negotiations of any substance, managers and others not directly involved are going to ask the participants about what has been agreed. Verbal versions, passed on several times, are liable to considerable distortion and the only remedy is the issue, rapidly, of a definitive and jointly-agreed statement.

Even in informal discussions, a quick note is often useful.

A production manager had a short meeting with the tool room shop steward about the operation of the quality bonus. They agreed a minor change to the system. As soon as the meeting had finished, the manager dictated a note:

'I am writing to confirm the outcome of our discussion this morning. You queried the method of calculating the scrap rate when substandard materials were discovered. I agreed that in future, rejects caused by such material would be discounted in the week in which they occurred instead of, as now, one week in arrears. The new system will start on 1 March.'

Note in this example, too, that a start date has been agreed and documented so that there can be no later misunderstanding. Not all negotiators recognize the importance of written confirmation.
This hands an advantage to the side which does, because they can volunteer to produce it. This is not to suggest that in drafting the note, distortions or new points can be introduced. That would risk justifiable criticism for deceit. Nevertheless, the party which drafts the agreement does have the advantage of choosing the precise wording, sequence and emphasis which it considers is the most satisfactory exposition of what has been agreed. So one's own side's leader can conclude the negotiation by saying: 'We ought to get this down on paper as quickly as possible: we'll produce a draft tomorrow morning and check it out with you by telephone.'

Avoiding 'fudge'

Towards the end of a long, difficult negotiation, when agreement has been half-hearted on some issues, while others have not really been grasped, there is a temptation to try to bring matters to a conclusion by agreeing a form of words which glosses over the difficult issues - in other words, the awkward points are fudged.

For example, a personnel manager had a difficult meeting with the office trade union representative about a variety of issues concerning working conditions and the use of new technology. Among these issues was the question of alleged over-crowding. After a whole day's not always constructive discussion, both sides wanted to close the meeting and go home. Most of the specific points had been agreed, but the over-crowding issue had barely been addressed.

The personnel manager persuaded the union representatives to accept a package statement about the whole negotiation which included this clause: 'In determining a revised office layout. the management will have regard to the union's view that the layout, as originally proposed, was not wholly adequate in terms of floor space.'

What did this mean? The personnel manager saw it as a sop to the union and a way of getting agreement on the other issues without committing the company to anything specific.

The union saw it as accepting their very precise floor space allocation claims. This misunderstanding eventually led to the agreement on the other issues coming unstuck, and a further dispute arising.

The risk of fudge is greatest when the negotiators are not the people who will have to put the agreement into practice - national pay negotiators, for example, who agree a loose form of words about overtime which then results in argument about their interpretation at local level. It is a risk, too, which may occur if lawyers for two companies act for their principals and are given too little guidance about the practicalities of implementation.

If the clear spelling out of an agreement means that one party or another withdraws its accord, the answer is to renegotiate the points of difficulty which have been revealed - not to attempt to gloss over them by an imprecise form of words.

Key points

• The final offer and agreement needs to be timed to coincide with a period of constructive discussion - not during a combative phase.
• It is important to achieve credibility for any statement about an offer being final - the tone and style of such a statement may be as important as its substance.
• Devices can be used to break a deadlock in reaching agreement - such as promises of future negotiations on a related topic, or making the introduction of a new condition subject to later review.
• Before finalizing an agreement, check that all aspects have been agreed, particularly dates for implementation, review or completion; and definitions of terms.
• Ensure full understanding of what has been agreed by final summaries and by producing written confirmation.
• Unresolved issues should not be 'fudged' by producing vague or ambiguous forms of words in order to achieve apparent agreement.

Chapter 13 - Securing Implementation

Reaching and documenting an agreement is not an end in itself. The purpose of any negotiation is to produce an outcome or action. In simple negotiations, the agreement and the outcome may coincide. Seller and buyer bargain about a price and immediately agreement is reached, the sale is affected. But in many cases there is delay between the close of negotiations and the agreed action taking place. There may be agreement, too, on what the outcome is to be, but no definition as to who has to do what in order to achieve this. During the period of delay between agreement and action, or because of lack of clarity about implementation, some agreements fail to achieve their intended results. Attention to implementation is, therefore, crucial if effective negotiation is to be translated into effective action.

Three elements in the process require particular attention:

• Including an implementation programme in the agreement.
• Establishing a joint implementation team.
• Ensuring adequate information and explanation to those affected by the agreement but not involved in the negotiations.

An agreed implementation programme

In any instance in which implementation of what has been agreed is not either immediate or wholly unambiguous, the last part of the negotiation itself should be devoted to agreeing what has to be done, and by whom, to ensure the agreement is affected.

George Jones, a company personnel manager, was handling a protracted and complex negotiation with a trade union team about new, flexible working hours. Agreement was eventually reached that instead of a fixed 39 hour week, the standard requirement would be for employees to work an average of *38* hours weekly, calculated over an eight week period during which actual hours might vary between 35 and 40, depending on production requirements. Unfortunately, both sides in the negotiation were so keen to conclude a deal after many wearisome hours of argument that the implementation -apart from a start date - was not discussed. A variety of problems then occurred as the managers and shop stewards who had not been involved directly in the negotiations – but who had to operate it on a day-to-day basis - began to place their own and differing interpretations on the agreement.

George subsequently had to reconvene the negotiating teams to hammer out these implementation details - only to be met by the trade unions saying that in the light of the difficulties which had occurred, they now wished to see a further reduction to a 37 hour average.

If George had included a detailed implementation plan as part of the original agreement it is probable that this attempt to re-negotiate would not have occurred.

The same principle applies even to informal, managerial discussions.

Too often, an agreement to do something is left hanging in mid-air without any definition of time-scales or action plans. The accountant eventually agrees to revise the production manager's costing system, but neither of them clarify when this revision is to be completed or whether the action lies wholly with the accountant.

Three questions need to be answered about any agreement in which implementation is not coincident or immediate:

• When is action to implement going to be started - and finished?
• What has to be done to achieve implementation?
• Who is to undertake this work?

Joint implementation

In many cases, action will need to be taken by both parties to an agreement. For example, in the case of the new working hours agreement, management will need to brief the supervisors and the union negotiators will need to brief the shop stewards. To ensure that both groups are given the same information, it may, therefore, be helpful to form a joint implementation team. Another example in a different setting emphasises the value in some circumstances of a joint approach to implementation:

A local authority wanted to review its senior management salary structure, and decided to seek outside assistance from a firm of management consultants. Three consultants were invited to submit proposals, and one was selected for the review - subject to satisfactory negotiation of a fee and detailed terms of reference. Having reached agreement on these issues, the discussion turned to implementation. How was the consultant actually to undertake the review? What action or input would be needed from the authority to help make the review most useful? It was eventually agreed that a joint review team would be the best solution, with one of the authority's personnel staff working with a consultant, both under the project direction of a senior consultant.

Joint implementation teams are also a common feature of major business development programmes in which, after initial negotiation about fees or financial contributions, the parties involved evolve a partnership approach to the management of the agreed project.

Information and explanation

Most industrial relations agreements depend for their success on the actions of possibly thousands of individual managers, supervisors and trade union representatives - none of whom took part in the actual negotiations. Explaining such agreements fully and clearly to all concerned in their implementation is essential. Even in a small company, a deal struck between the chairman and the local union organizer needs to be explained to the supervisors and staff.

It is in this phase that imprecise wording in the original agreement (the 'fudge' referred to in an earlier chapter) can be very damaging. A phrase such as 'the company will take such reasonable steps as are practicable to reduce the risk of vehicle accidents within its premises' will be interpreted in widely different ways by different people - a potent source of dispute as to whether or not the agreement is being honoured.

Too often, information about agreements is limited to the issue of badly drafted notices, or to word-of-mouth messages which become progressively distorted as they pass down the management chain.

Any agreement of substance or complexity which involves people not involved in the original negotiation merits a carefully designed and executed programme of information and explanation. Another common fault in the industrial relations field is for each side independently to issue its own explanation - and for these explanations to differ. Joint agreement to explanatory information, or the issue of such information on a joint basis, is highly desirable. Again, several questions should be asked:

• Who needs to know about this agreement if it is to be implemented effectively?
• What do they need to know?
• How is this information best communicated (eg written or verbal)?

- By whom?
- Within what time-scales?

Key points

- An agreement is not successful until it has been effectively implemented.
- It is often helpful to include an implementation programme as an integral part of a negotiated agreement.
- An implementation programme defines what has to be done, when and by whom.
- For some agreements, implementation may be best effected by a joint team.
- Those affected by, or required to apply, an agreement (though not involved in the actual negotiation) need adequate information and explanation.
- Such action should be based on defining who needs to know what, how and by whom this information should be given, by what methods and to what time-scales.

Chapter 14 - Handling Breakdown

Negotiations are not always successful, and the wise negotiator gives prior thought to what action might be needed if agreement cannot be achieved. Contingency planning of this kind is not defeatist. It merely accepts the uncertainties of the bargaining process and ensures that thought is given to the consequences of breakdown *before,* rather than after the event.

Reviewing what would happen if the negotiation is unsuccessful may also influence the bargaining tactics and objectives. It may be realized, for example, that in the event of breakdown, the other party will probably take legal action and that one's own position at law is relatively weak. In such circumstances, it would be unwise to set too high a target. Alternatively, the breakdown of negotiations with, say, a supplier, may mean only that new negotiations will then have to be opened with an alternative source of supply.

The questions to ask before negotiations begin are therefore:

If agreement cannot be concluded:

• Can the matter be resolved by taking unilateral action?
• Is it feasible to maintain the status quo as an alternative to what was being pursued in the negotiation?
• Has the other party the power to inflict damage (e.g. industrial action, or commercial veto)?
• Can the other side unilaterally refer the matter to a third party, such as the courts or an arbitrator?
• Should arbitration or legal action be considered as an option for one's own side?
• If referred to a third party, is the outcome likely to be less favourable than one's bottom limit?
• Might third party assistance in the form of conciliation or mediation be helpful?

The main options are to take unilateral action or to use third party intervention - which can be of two kinds, conciliation (or mediation) and arbitration. These are discussed in more detail below.

Unilateral action

A general rule has been suggested in an earlier chapter: do not negotiate if the outcome can be achieved by direct action. On this basis, there is no option for opposition to the parties to be resolved by unilateral action since negotiations would not have been embarked on in the first place. But like most rules, there can be exceptions.

For example, in industrial relations there may be many circumstances in which an employer has the power to impose changes in working conditions, but on which it is normal to seek agreement with the trade unions. An agreed solution is much more likely to be implemented effectively than one which, by its imposition, generates employee resentment. There are parallel situations in many informal managerial interactions. The finance director may have the authority to require line managers to submit a new type of expenditure return, but may also feel it wiser to negotiate their agreement to the change rather than to impose it. In most instances of this kind, however, the option of exercising ultimate power or authority is one which needs to be retained.

Whether or not to use it has to be a matter of judgement in the particular circumstances and points to consider will be:

• What will be the effect of imposition on the quality of the relationship with the other party?
• Has the other party the power and the will to be obstructive, even if not wholly able to prevent implementation of the imposed solution?

• Will any damage caused by a reaction to imposition be worse than either dropping the matter and retaining the status quo, or a reference to third party intervention?

Third party intervention

An analysis of the realities of breakdown may indicate that it would be unwise to proceed unilaterally, or that one has no power to do so. It may also be unacceptable or impossible for the position existing before the negotiation started, to continue. In such circumstances, third party intervention may be a useful option to consider. There are two main forms of third party involvement, though each has two variants:

• Conciliation or mediation

In these forms, the third party does not produce a binding decision but works with the parties in dispute to help them reach agreement.

The conciliator ensures that the two parties are not misunderstanding each other, and that they have considered all possible angles. The emphasis is on helping them evolve their *own* agreed solution, not on the production of solutions by the conciliator.

The mediator is expected to go further and, after listening to the two sides, to suggest solutions. Neither party, however, is under a formal obligation to accept the mediator's proposals.

• Arbitration or court rulings

Here, the third party (arbitrator or a court or tribunal) considers the arguments of both parties and then produces a binding solution or ruling.

Whether arbitration is an option will depend on whether prior and joint agreement exists about its use: without such agreement (or provision for arbitration being contractual) it is not normally open for one party to impose the use of an arbitrator on the other. Ideally, both parties agree, before negotiation begins, that if they fail to reach agreement the matter will be referred to arbitration and each will abide by the arbitrator's decision.

The position is different where use of the legal system (courts or tribunals) is concerned. Here, it is open for one party to pursue a legal claim whether or not the other wishes the matter to be dealt with in this way. The courts can, of course, be used only to resolve issues lying within the purview of statute or common law and the most frequent use of the law is to deal with contractual disputes and with claims for damages or compensation.

Different forms of conciliation and arbitration exist in different types of negotiation, and these are mentioned in each of the next three chapters. Three short examples are given here to illustrate more generally the situations in which various types of third party intervention need to be considered as part of negotiating strategy:

William Scott, a factory production superintendent, had agreed to the request of Gerry Wickens, a superintendent of another section, to take on transfer an employee with whom there had been a personality clash. But after three months, Scott also found the employee difficult to deal with and told Wickens he would have to take him back. After a long discussion, Wickens refused. Scott knew he had no authority to insist on the transfer back, but felt, too, that the present position was untenable. Some form of intervention by a third party was his only way forward and he had to decide whether he would seek conciliation by the personnel manager, or a ruling (in effect, arbitration) from the factory manager. His choice was influenced by his assessment of the likely outcomes.

He thought the personnel manager would be sympathetic to his position, and was renowned for her persuasive abilities. The factory manager, on the other hand, might well take the view that having accepted the employee knowing him to be a difficult case, Scott was stuck with the result and must live with it. So he suggested to Wickens, who agreed, that they should explain the problem to the personnel manager and seek her advice.

A local Council had let a contract to a construction company to build a town swimming pool. Shortly after contract completion, and before final payments had been made, the filtration system broke down and the pool's opening had to be delayed for several weeks while remedial work was done. As a result, the council lost considerable income from swimming fees, and decided to claim compensation from the main contractor. The contractor blamed the breakdown on financial constraints imposed by the council which allegedly resulted in a different and cheaper filtration system being installed than the contractor considered desirable. Negotiations failed to resolve the dispute. However, the contract provided for a reference of any dispute to arbitration, which was how the matter was finally settled - to the satisfaction of the council. The council's negotiating objectives were decided in the light of this enforceable reference to arbitration, and an assessment that the council had a strong case. The council, consequently, gave very little ground in the preliminary negotiations in order to avoid prejudicing their case at arbitration.

There was a small publishing company. The ten journalists (but not the rest of the staff) were union members, and it was normal for the chief executive to conclude an annual wage agreement with the journalists. On one occasion, they claimed a 10 per cent increase at a time when the going rate in the industry was just over 5 per cent. Negotiations resulted in the union lowering their claim to 9 per cent and the company offering 6 per cent, but no agreement could be reached. The chief executive then said that he was considering imposing a 6 per cent settlement - which he thought the non-union staff would be very pleased with - but was willing to consider using the services of a non-executive director as a mediator. The union agreed, and the director was asked to consider the views of both sides and then to suggest what the increase should be. Neither the chief executive nor the union agreed in advance to accept the mediating director's proposals, but in the event, his eventual suggestion of a 7 per cent award was accepted.

Conciliation comes closest to normal negotiation and carries the least risk of matters being taken out of one's control. It does not, however, put the other side under heavy pressure to compromise and may not, therefore, be enough to shift the other party from a heavily entrenched position.

Mediation places the parties under much stronger psychological pressure - but short of enforcement - to accept a solution which may be significantly worse than the bottom line.

In arbitration, both parties give up control of the outcome and the risk, therefore, exists of having a position imposed which hitherto has been considered unacceptable. A very thorough and realistic assessment of the validity of one's own position and arguments is, therefore, essential before either agreeing to arbitration, or allowing negotiations to reach an impasse from which enforceable arbitration or legal action is the only course open to the other side. A common failing is to be over-optimistic about the validity or strength of one's own case, or to underestimate the other party's position. Assessing the weak points in one's own case is of almost more importance than recognizing its strengths.

Key points

- Giving thought to the situation which would occur if the negotiations failed to achieve agreement is an essential part of planning for negotiation.
- It is unwise to allow a negotiation to fail if the probable outcome - whether because of action by the other party or through third party intervention – is worse than the position reached when breakdown occurs.
- The main options of handling breakdown are to take unilateral action to enforce an outcome, or to seek third party intervention.
- In considering unilateral action, thought needs to be given to the effect of such action on future working relationships.

- The least extreme form of third party assistance is conciliation, in which a conciliator works with the two parties to help them reach agreement.
- A more direct form is mediation, in which both parties agree to consider (but are not bound to accept) a solution suggested by the mediator.
- The most powerful and risky form of third party resolution is arbitration - where both parties bind themselves in advance to accept the arbitrator's solution - or legal action through the courts or tribunals.
- Making sound decisions about the use of conciliation, mediation or arbitration depends on thorough and accurate assessments of the strength of each party's case.

Chapter 15 - Negotiating by Letter and Phone

Negotiation is normally thought of as a verbal process - a to and fro of discussion, argument, question and answer between two people or two teams meeting face-to-face. So far, documentation has been considered in this book only in relation to the confirmation of the final agreement in writing. Direct verbal discussion is by far the most common negotiating mode, but there are occasions in which correspondence or the telephone can play a useful part, or may even be used as an alternative to a conventional face-to-face meeting.

Negotiating by correspondence

It is not uncommon for commercial and industrial relations negotiations to begin with an exchange of letters, even if these consist of no more than a request for a meeting and confirmation of its time and place. These letters may, though, be used in an attempt to establish an opening position or to set the tone for later negotiation. They should certainly be considered as an integral element of the whole process and not merely as preliminary administration. This point has long been recognized by solicitors, whose initial letters registering, say, their clients' claims for compensation may be designed to jolt the recipients into taking the matter seriously, or to undermine their complacency. Trade unions, too, use this technique.

Alan Dickens, personnel manager of a distribution company, received a letter from Sue Macklin, the union district organizer.

It said: 'We are seeking an urgent meeting to discuss the very grave situation which has arisen in the despatch department due to management's failure to supply our members with protective footwear. There has been a blatant breach of safety legislation and of the company's safety agreement. If immediate action is not forthcoming, we will have to consider what action is open to us, such as a report to the Health and Safety Executive.' This letter was clearly designed to make the company sit up and take notice: to create a tone of urgency and importance. It was much more than merely a written request for a meeting; it was part of the negotiation itself.

The experienced negotiator will recognize a ploy of this kind and will make a judgement about the best form of response. Of course, if the urgency in the opening letter is justified, the best move will probably be to agree to a very early meeting. But if it is thought that a tactic is being used to bolster an otherwise weak or unimportant issue, the negotiation might be continued by letter.

In this case, that is what Alan Dickens did. He wrote back, saying: 'We are certainly willing to arrange a meeting should this prove necessary, but to avoid any waste of time it would be helpful if you would first let me have a note of whatever action the despatch department's shop steward has taken to resolve the matter within the department. Perhaps you could also explain whether your reference to safety shoes refers to the loading bay, as we have no record of any previous discussions about this subject for any other section.'
This letter put the ball back in the union's court. There was a two week delay until a further letter was received, giving more specific details of the complaint. The delay, and the receipt of the second letter, enabled Dickens to conduct his own investigation and to prepare a constructive response - also by letter - which resolved what was, in fact. a minor matter without a meeting having to take place.

Although in many instances it would be unwise or unsatisfactory to attempt to conduct negotiations solely by correspondence, there are situations in which such a course may offer some advantages over face-to-face meetings:

• Much time may be saved. Negotiating meetings are notoriously time-consuming, even when minor matters are being considered. In the case just quoted, it is not improbable that a meeting involving perhaps two managers and three trade union officials would have lasted a couple of hours. Producing two or three letters and reading the replies took less than half this time.
• It may be possible to avoid an otherwise emotionally charged meeting and deal with the problem much more rationally. It may be known that a manager or trade union official is an excitable or belligerent negotiator at meetings. Dealing with an issue through correspondence may elicit a more reasonable response.
• The negotiation will be on record - which may be an important point if there is a possibility of eventual legal action.
• If very complex proposals are involved, putting them in writing should help to eliminate the risk of misunderstanding which can sometimes arise in the heat of verbal negotiation. Time can be given to the very careful drafting of a written proposal (or response to the other party's position), and this is not subject to the immediate challenge or even interruption which can occur in a meeting.

In practice, a mixture of written and verbal negotiation is often the best procedure. The negotiations may start with a short exchange of letters in which both parties clarify their intentions. A meeting or meetings then take place. One party may then suggest an adjournment for a few days while they review the position, and follow this with a letter setting out detailed proposals which are then the subject of further direct negotiation. Eventually an agreement is reached which is confirmed in writing.

Negotiating by telephone

Lengthy or complex negotiations cannot be conducted on the telephone
but there are occasions when this mode of negotiation is extremely effective. There is something about the telephone which encourages at least some people to be more co-operative than in face-to-face discussions. The unplanned or unexpected nature of a phone call, which may interrupt higher priority work, sometimes reduces the care and resistance which is usually exercised in face-to-face negotiation.

The local manager of a security firm telephoned the administration manager of a client company and asked for a meeting to discuss possible alterations to the detail of the contract for night security services. Instead of fixing a date for a meeting. the administration manager said: 'I have a very heavy diary over the next couple of weeks: have you got a few minutes to talk about it on the phone now?' In the resultant telephone discussion, the security company's proposals were quickly modified and an alternative revision agreed - subject to written confirmation. The security manager later commented, somewhat ruefully, that he should have insisted on a meeting as he found himself agreeing to the administration manager's counter-proposals far too readily.

Another case illustrates many managers' experience that points of detail which can involve lengthy discussion at a meeting, may be agreed very quickly on the telephone:

A company personnel manager had just concluded a very long negotiation with the white-collar trade union about revisions to car allowances. He then realized that both parties had omitted to deal with the small number of staff who were paid a motor cycle allowance. Should he reconvene the meeting?

He decided not to. Instead, he phoned the union official and said: 'We need to round off the car allowance agreement by an adjustment to the motor cycle figures. I've checked the latest statistics and an increase of 3p per mile seems justified. Is this OK with you?' To which the answer, after a very short pause for thought. was Yes. The personnel manager was relieved at this rapid resolution, as he remembered a lengthy argument about these payments at the previous year's negotiating meeting.

There is a danger, of course, that such attempts at quick deals will misfire; that the answer will be No. Negotiators who try to get quick results by using the telephone need to be reasonably confident that their opposite numbers have less skill in the use of this particular mode of bargaining.

Key points

• Face-to-face discussions are not the only form of negotiation: effective use can also be made of correspondence and the telephone.
• An opening letter can help to set the parameters and style of later negotiation.
• All or part of a negotiation, dealt with by correspondence, may save time, avoid an emotional confrontation, provide a record of the negotiation, and enable carefully drafted and complex proposals to be produced.
• Some negotiators are less resistant to proposals when discussing them on the telephone.
• Telephone discussions may be used to settle minor or simple negotiating points extremely quickly.

Chapter 16 - Handling the Media

Newspapers, radio and television have always been interested in major industrial relations issues - particularly when negotiations break down and strikes occur. Similar interest is shown in some highly publicized commercial battles. In recent years there have been two related developments which have brought more managers into contact with the media than just the heads of major national or international companies:

• A growth in local radio and television has resulted in even quite small-scale negotiations being covered by news stories and interviews. A dispute about impending redundancies in a local factory, or news of the negotiation of the sale of a piece of land for a new hotel, are the types of incident which help to make up the daily diet of local journalists.
• To an increasing extent, companies are actively using the media - whether through advertisements or interviews - as a channel of communication to influence the outcome of commercial and industrial relations negotiations. Instead of just responding, often reluctantly, to media requests for statements, they are commissioning public relations and advertising consultants to advise on how the media can be used to promote their negotiating objectives, or to gain public understanding and support.

Negotiations themselves cannot be conducted through press or television, but in some situations thought needs to be given to the active use of the media as a channel of communication and influence; and to the response to be given to media requests for news and comment about negotiating issues which are of public interest.
If a manager becomes involved in media comment, or if it is decided to issue statements or notices to the media, the two main aspects to consider are:

- The characteristics of effective media communication
- The choice of media and method of communication.

Effective media communication

It needs to be recognized that in any use of the media, two audiences are involved - the other party to the negotiation or dispute, and the public at large. Public opinion can have a significant effect, particularly on employees during a strike. A feeling that public support has been lost undermines strikers' morale - and the converse is also true. So one aim of media messages is to influence public attitudes.

In doing this, though, it must be remembered that while the public may not be able to spot errors or distortions in a story, those directly involved will, and that this may well generate an even firmer resolve by the other party to continue their resistance. There are, then, three main characteristics of effective media communications:

- *Accuracy:* facts and figures should be accurate and capable of being proved right if challenged. While some selectivity or simplification is often necessary, this should not be so blatant as to lead to justifiable charges of distortion and omission.
- *Clarity:* however complex or technical the issues, the language (written or spoken) must be simple, direct and understandable to the lay person.
- *Reasonableness:* whatever the provocation, it is desirable to promote an impression of solid common-sense and sweet reason - not rancour or rhetoric.

These points are illustrated in the following examples of the use of different media.

The choice of media and method

There are a number of ways of getting one's case into the public domain:

press advertisements
press conferences
radio or TV interviews.
press releases
news stories
media interviews

Press advertisements

There is only one way to retain total control over the wording and presentation of a message and avoid any editorial cutting - to buy advertising space. It is a method used increasingly by large employers during industrial disputes, by major companies involved in takeover battles, and by bodies wanting to influence their negotiations with government.
If total control is the advantage, then the disadvantage is that the advertisement carries less weight with the public (and perhaps the other party) than news stories or editorial comment.
Advertisements are taken with a pinch of salt. Their most effective use is probably to give very straightforward information, rather than views or comment.

In one lengthy local dispute. about 500 factory employees went on strike over plans to introduce new shift work schedules. The strike was unofficial. and included a number of employees who - so far as the company knew - were not union members. It was far from clear that communications to the strikers through the union office would be passed on to all those involved. And because of high labour turnover the company was not confident that its records of home addresses were wholly reliable. Yet a point was reached when it was necessary to get a message across to all the employees. A full-page advertisement was. therefore. placed in both local papers. addressed very specifically to the employees on strike. saying in very unambiguous terms that everyone who reported for work on the following Monday morning would be able to resume work without any detriment to holiday pay; but that anyone not so reporting would be deemed to have resigned.

The wisdom of such an ultimatum might be open to question: what was undisputed was that the message did get across to all concerned. Even those who read neither paper had it quickly drawn to their attention by relatives or friends.

Press releases

A press release is a prepared statement which is issued to newspapers, radio and television for them to use or not as they think fit.

Like the advertisement, it has the merit of being a statement which is, at least initially, under the control of the initiator - but there the resemblance ends. The media are under no obligation to print the statement as it stands, or at all. It may be ignored, because it is considered un-newsworthy. It may be reproduced in full. Often, however, it will be used merely as the basis for a news story written by journalists who may quote selectively from it. It can be frustrating in the extreme - and may be damaging to one's negotiating interests

- to find just one phrase from a carefully prepared statement embedded in a not wholly accurate news story.

To stand the best chance of being used with minimum editorial interference, press releases should be clear, concise, and written in the same style as the media concerned use in their own news stories.

One idea, often employed successfully, is to personalize the message by giving it as a quote from a named person.

The first draft of a press release, produced by a company production manager about an industrial dispute read:

'Messrs AMD Ltd regret to announce that despite their offer to the unions to resolve the current dispute by consolidating attendance allowances within the bonus calculator, thus generating a multiplying effect on the already generous production bonus, it proved impossible at a meeting this morning to persuade the unions to terminate their industrial action.'

The company's press officer hastily rewrote this as:

'Speaking at the end of a long meeting with trade union secretary John Brown this morning, Adrian Green, AMD's production manager said: 'We're almost at the end of the line in this dispute. We upped the value of our offer from about 5 per cent to a package worth nearly 8 per cent when better bonuses are taken into account. but the union wouldn't budge an inch. They say the strike goes on. We think it's about time they gave their members a chance to say what they think about this much improved offer.'

This statement was reproduced word for word in the local paper and on local radio. It helped the company's local reputation and played a part in influencing the employees to put pressure on the union officials to call a mass meeting to consider the company's new offer.

Press conferences

On an issue for which maximum publicity is sought - perhaps to generate public opposition to a local authority's planning decision which has been the subject of abortive negotiation - the issue of a press release or official statement can be combined with a press conference. Media journalists are invited to attend, with the lure of a promise of a newsworthy statement being made, followed by a question and answer session.

To ensure a good attendance, it is best to fix a venue convenient to the media, such as a town centre hotel. It is also normal to provide light (or liquid) refreshments, and to say so when issuing the invitations to attend.

The advantage of a press conference is that it provides an opportunity to provide much more information and explanation than can be given in a short press release. There are three possible disadvantages or risks:

• That no one may attend as a result of other more immediate news items taking editorial priority on the day.
• That the questioning may be hostile, or concentrate on issues which are not central to the case the company wants to make.
• That no control whatsoever can be exercised over the news stories which may be written. Busy journalists or sub-editors may limit the story they print to just one item in what was a quite complex statement or discussion; this is likely to be what the media consider newsworthy and which may be peripheral to the company's case.

News stories

A less formal, and often more successful, way of getting the organization's case into the media is to telephone the relevant news desk, say there is a story to tell, and invite a journalist to listen - either on the phone or by meeting. Any resultant story is likely to be written as a straightforward news item, rather than as an account of a company-initiated news event. It may, therefore, carry more credibility with the readers.

Organizations employing press or public relations officers ensure that good relationships are cultivated with a few key journalists who can be relied on to listen to a company story, and if they consider it newsworthy, to write it up fairly.

Media interviews

In other instances, it is the media who initiate contact with the organization, asking for information or comment. Such approaches can range from the informal telephone call from the local paper, asking for an immediate comment, to a pre-arranged interview on radio or TV. All such contacts, however informal, need to be handled with care. The telephone call from a journalist needs particular care. It is by no means uncommon for a manager to treat such a call as a relatively casual matter, with the skilled journalist adopting a very friendly, conversational rather than interrogative manner. The manager may not realize that what is said may be quoted verbatim, and built up into a major story.

The personnel officer of a K-Cloth, a small clothing factory, was phoned by a local reporter at the time of high refugees. There had been some initial union opposition to offering employment to the refugees, but negotiations had eventually resulted in agreement. 'I hear you're taking on some of the refugees as machinists', said the reporter. The personnel officer was very ready to confirm this and the conversation developed into a general chat about the plight of the boat people. The reporter was just about to ring off when she said, apparently still conversationally rather than as part of an interview: 'Incidentally, I hear that eight of the maintenance staff are being made redundant', to which the personnel officer replied: 'Yes. We've been a bit overstaffed there and are having to cut our overhead costs.' 'Thanks: said the reporter, 'It's been nice talking to you.' The personnel officer was horrified the following day to see, as the front page headline on the local paper: 'K-CLOTH SACK 8 LOCALS: HIRE 10 REFUGEES'.

The essential requirement, when telephoned by a journalist, is to check the status of the conversation before giving any information or making any comment. 'Are you getting background, or is this discussion for the record?' is the question to ask: and even then to be very cautious about saying anything which if quoted out of context might damage the organization's case.
More time is available to consider what one wants to say in prearranged radio or TV interviews. It is normal, too, before the interview starts, for the interviewer to outline the intended subject matter of his or her questions. But this is no safeguard against the unexpectedly awkward question.

The manager of a port authority was interviewed on the local TV network about the dock strike. The interviewer explained in advance that he would be asking about the employer's views of the effect of the strike on jobs, and about the action the employers might have to take to protect their business.

However, the manager was visibly disconcerted by the very first question in the interview itself which was: 'When are you going to begin sacking the employees who are now on strike?'

The key to handling such interviews successfully is to decide in advance on the one or two (no more) important points to be got across, regardless of what questions are asked. Good interviewees are not passive respondents who allow the interviewer to control the style and scope of the verbal exchange. A media interview is neither a test of the ability to say as little as possible under interrogation, nor an occasion to feed the interviewer with the replies which, from a media viewpoint, make good television. It is an opportunity to communicate one's case to a very wide audience. The interviewer is, in practice, very unlikely to ask the ideal question from the interviewee's viewpoint. One needs, therefore, to prepare a short, crisp statement, encapsulating the most important point to be made, and think how this can be given in response to whatever question might be asked.

Take the example of Adrian Green of AMD, referred to earlier in this chapter. Interviewed on local TV after issuing the press statement. he was asked: 'M r Green, you were not able to settle the strike at your meeting this morning: what are you going to do next?' His reply, prepared in advance as an all purpose answer to almost any question, was 'The real issue is when is the union going to allow their members to have a say about the company's latest offer.' It was an answer which, with very little amendment, could have been given to almost any question which he might have been asked, and it concentrated on the message which Green wanted to register both with the public and with his employees.

In this, and the other examples given in this chapter, handling the media skillfully - whether in response to media interest or by taking the initiative - does not by itself resolve any specific negotiating difficulty. Media news and comment can, though, influence attitudes and thus have a potentially powerful effect on the resolve of those involved, and on the degree of support or opposition which they experience from the public at large.

Key points

• Negotiations cannot be conducted through the media, but the media can be used to influence the attitudes of those concerned, and - where appropriate - public understanding and support.
• The common characteristics of media communications of all kinds are accuracy, clarity and reasonableness.
• Press advertisements offer full control over what is said, but their status as advertisements may reduce their credibility.
• Press releases provide initial control over content, but it cannot be guaranteed that they will be reproduced fully, or at all.
• Press releases need to be written in the style of the media to which they are issued.
• Journalists may be assisted or persuaded to write news stories. These may carry more public credibility than company statements, but incur the risk of error or distortion.
• Radio or TV interviews should be seen as opportunities to put across a message in clear, simple terms, regardless of the precise questions which are asked.

Chapter 17 - Influencing Managerial Negotiations

In previous chapters, negotiation has been considered as an activity which occurs in many different contexts, and examples have been drawn from formal and informal negotiations, and from managerial, commercial and industrial relations settings. In this and the next two chapters, the specific characteristics of each of these three settings is examined in more detail. The question being dealt with is: what features of each setting influence the nature and success of negotiation in that context? In this chapter we look at the informal negotiating interactions between managers which are an integral element of the whole management process. The general factor is that managers have working relationships which extend beyond the scope of any single issue. Their ability to influence each other in any specific negotiating episode will, therefore, be affected by the nature and quality of their general relationships. There are four particular major influences at work here:

- The relative status of the managers involved
- Connections with sources of power in the organization
- The creation of obligations
- The power of knowledge and expertise.

Status

Almost all organizations operate through management hierarchies, and the relative status of managers who are trying to influence each other has a marked effect on the outcome of their discussions.

Interaction between senior managers and their direct line subordinates cannot really be described as negotiation, because the seniors have ultimate authority to make decisions and override their subordinates' views. Power, in other words, is extremely one-sided.

That is not to say that many negotiating skills cannot be used to good effect by a subordinate who is trying to persuade his or her line manager to a particular line of action. But the ultimate right of the boss to make the final decision distinguishes this type of managerial interaction from real negotiation.

The situation is different when managers from different parts of an organization meet for discussions - and this type of managerial contact occupies more of many managers' time than boss/subordinate meetings. Here, neither manager can exercise executive authority over the other. The outcome of discussions should depend on their skills of argument and persuasion. Where two managers' status is perceived as equal, this is very much the case. So when the chief accountant meets the chief buyer to suggest that a change to purchasing schedules would reduce the cost of stock holdings – and both are at the same hierarchical level - the outcome will depend largely on their respective negotiating ability.

Suppose, though, that a meeting of this kind takes place between two managers of different status. The chief accountant may, for example, have sent a section accountant (a lower managerial level) to talk to the chief buyer. In this case, the status difference may have an unspoken effect. The chief buyer may feel more confident to express opposition; the accountant may feel inhibited in pressing the case as strongly as the chief accountant would have done. There are some senior managers who exploit status differences quite crudely, but this type of status influence is often quite subtle. It may not even occur to the senior of the two that the other and less senior manager is being inhibited by having to deal with someone at a higher level in the hierarchy. The following example illustrates this:

A local authority chief executive set up a working party to plan the reorganization and re-equipment of the central administrative offices. The members of the working party were drawn from the finance, office services and personnel departments.

The four members of the finance and office services departments were all 'third tier' staff (two levels below the heads of the departments) paid on a senior management grade. The single personnel department representative was a 'fifth tier' training officer, on a much lower management grade.

The working party's final recommendations, though generally very sound, were found in practice to have underestimated the volume of office staff training required to operate the new word-processing equipment. The training officer on the working party was asked by his boss to explain why he had not ensured that training was given adequate attention. The training officer replied that he had recognized this weakness in the working party's deliberations before its recommendations were finalized. 'But', he went on, 'I became aware at around this time that I was the most junior member of the working party. I think this prevented me from arguing as forcibly as I should have done for more attention to be given to staff training.'

Two lessons arise from this example:

• For senior managers, the message is never to underestimate the effect of status differences on the confidence of junior staff, including those in other departments than their own. If a positive contribution is looked for from a junior manager, equally positive encouragement and support may need to be given to overcome the inhibiting influence of status.

• For junior managers, the message is to think through the issue positively and to realize that in managerial discussions outside the direct executive line, their ability to negotiate effectively stems from other factors than status - and particularly by the expertise they can demonstrate in relation to the subject under discussion.

Connections with sources of power

Just as status can be used manipulatively by a senior to 'squash' a junior opponent, so the juniors may be able to use the existence of their connections with other powerful managers as a manipulative response. This is not a very attractive feature of managerial life: in an ideal world all managerial negotiations would be resolved as a result of a rational and impersonal analysis of the issues. But if an able young manager is faced with manipulative opposition, the use of connections may become necessary. The point can be illustrated by the case of a young woman manager who was being obstructed by a prejudiced and status-conscious older senior male manager:

Anne Stone was the newly-appointed personnel officer of a manufacturing company which had recently been taken over by a large conglomerate. The new chief executive, Bill Fraser, wanted to introduce a whole range of modern management techniques, with a particular emphasis on systematic performance appraisal.
He had selected Anne for her job largely because of her previous work as a management trainer in which she had specialized in appraisal training. He had also told her - though this was not known by other managers - that she would have his wholehearted backing in putting in an appraisal system, though he wanted this 'sold' to the managers, rather than imposed.

Anne succeeded in generating interest and support for a training programme as a precursor to the new system with all the managers but one - George Garnet. the crusty, 58-yearold production manager. At her meetings with him, he persisted in dealing with her ideas in a flippant manner, emphasized that as a member of the senior management team (which Anne was not) he knew what was needed better than she did, and generally indicated that he could not take the ideas of a young, more junior and woman manager seriously.

There came a stage at which all but Garnet's staff were scheduled for the training courses, while he still prevaricated about their involvement. Anne felt she had no alternative but to use the support she knew she would get from Bill Fraser but she wanted to avoid a direct appeal for his help. She took an opportunity one lunchtime of sharing a table with Fraser in the staff canteen. The following morning she made a point of running across Garnet in the factory. 'I was having lunch with Bill yesterday.' she said, 'And he was asking whether all departments had yet signed up for the appraisal training course. Can I expect your nominations this week?' This set Garnet's alarm bells ringing. 'Bill' he noted, not 'Mr Fraser'. Perhaps this young woman carried more managerial clout than he had realized, and his training nominations were rapidly forthcoming.

This is, of course, a somewhat crude example of the power of connections.

Normally, things do not have to be spelled out or hinted at so directly. A manager's connections with power sources become known and are then an unspoken influence on managerial negotiations.

What they do is alter the power balance, and they are, therefore, of particular importance for the manager who is otherwise in a weak bargaining position. The danger is that they can be used to support weak arguments, and may, therefore, result in poor decisions being made. Further, managers who use their informal contacts with power sources in an obviously manipulative manner generate much personal resentment. They may also be disowned by the seniors with whom they claim connections if they exploit such relationships too openly.

That said, it is still advisable in many managerial negotiations to be aware of informal power groupings and connections. Who has links with whom? From whom might someone obtain support? Assessments of all aspects of relative strength are necessary if bargaining expectations are to be realistic.

Obligations

Negotiations between managers may be quite strongly influenced by the general quality of their working and personal relationships – a factor which distinguishes this form of negotiation from many commercial or legal transactions in which the interacting parties meet only in the context of the negotiations. If the general relationship between managers is friendly, constructive and based on mutual respect for each other's expertise, then their negotiations will be equally soundly based. The outcomes will derive far more from a rational assessment of the issues than from considerations of status, connections or point-scoring.

The converse is, unfortunately, also true: that if a working relationship is tainted by personal rivalry, any negotiating episode is likely to be treated as a conflict in which concern about winning or losing will take precedence over producing effective, agreed solutions.

Some managers, aware of the strong influence of personal factors, set out deliberately to create a sense of obligation among their colleagues. They will be very helpful on issues which are not of major concern to them in order to build up a stock of goodwill which they can call on when their turn comes to seek something from other managers. So a manager may offer to assist a colleague whose section is temporarily short-staffed, not out of a genuinely collaborative attitude, but to create a sense of obligation to influence a later negotiating episode.

An ambitious, newly-appointed chief fire officer in a local authority was developing plans to achieve more autonomy in staff management matters. For this, he knew he would have to overcome resistance from the personnel director. Keeping his plans under wraps at this stage, he set out to 'cultivate' the personnel director by all possible means.
In management team meetings, he gave the personnel director strong support on several issues (not affecting the fire service) in which the latter's plans were being attacked by other senior managers. He also began inviting the personnel director and his wife to attend fire service social functions, offering to provide a fire service car and driver. Invitations for such functions had not been made by his predecessor.

Fortunately, the personnel director spotted this attempt to create obligations at a very early stage, and found reasons politely to decline any This example makes the point that the wise manager, while determined to establish constructive and friendly working relationships, is very wary of accepting unsolicited gifts (actual or metaphoric) however innocent such offers may seem. If a sense of obligation is a powerful influence on managerial bargaining, the only effective counter is to avoid obligations being created.

The power of expertise

The influence which stems from a manager's expertise on the matter under debate is a powerful and constructive counter to the negative, manipulative influences discussed earlier in this chapter. Young or more junior managers may find their negotiating positions on particular issues undermined by the wiles of older and more senior managers who have developed the skills of organizational politics.

But in the longer term, managers - whatever their age or status - who can demonstrate a mastery of their subject and an ability to apply this to organizational issues, will succeed in becoming influential in inter-managerial discussions and bargaining.

Not that the mere possession of knowledge and ideas is sufficient: the manager has to develop the ability to project these into the discussion in a way which makes an impact on the other participants. Partly, this involves acquiring a positive verbal style and the confidence, if it becomes necessary, to interrupt a discussion with a firm correction or interjection. Men, as well as women managers, may benefit from assertiveness training to help them overcome an initial tendency to be over-cautious about taking issue in a discussion.

Two other methods of gaining attention and providing a focus to a discussion are:

• To distribute a document or chart which either highlights the key points or provides supporting evidence. So in a discussion about measures to improve recruitment, in which differences of view exist about the costs of job advertising, a document showing an analysis of the response rates of different advertising media may focus the discussion on specific, rather than generalized, factors. It may also assist an otherwise unassertive manager to stress a case for which a purely verbal presentation has not yet made much impact.

• To use a flip chart to write up key points, or to chart the logic of the case being made. Obviously, a flip chart or wall board cannot be used so spontaneously as a document, but where such use can be arranged, the user can exercise considerable control over the whole structure of the meeting. An otherwise unassertive or nervous negotiator can also gain much confidence from speaking to a prepared brief, and ensuring that key points are registered by writing them up as the discussion proceeds.

There is one important point to watch when the strength of one's negotiating position is based almost wholly on the knowledge and expertise one can bring to the issue under discussion. This is, to ensure that what one puts forward is *correct.* A cynical, though successful, manager once said that there are two conditions which should govern any claimed statement (or statistic) of fact; either that if someone checks, the statement will be found to be correct; or that no-one can check it! Without going this far, it is evident that credibility and influence based on knowledge and expertise will be wholly undermined by any mistake or incorrect claim made on the basis of such knowledge. So the message is, prepare the case, check and double check the facts, and then display this know-how positively and confidently. That way, even the most junior of managers will gain respect and be able to influence the outcome of negotiations with more senior managers.

Key points

• Managerial negotiations are affected by the quality of managers' general working relationships.
• Junior managers may be inhibited by, and manipulative senior managers may exploit, differences of formal status between participants in managerial discussions.

• A participant's known or assumed personal contacts or connections with powerful individuals or groups may result in his or her negotiating position being given more credibility than would otherwise be the case.

• Manipulative managers attempt to create a sense of obligation - which wise managers resist - in order to influence later negotiations.

• The manipulative aspects of managerial negotiations can be countered by the powerful influence of knowledge and expertise which is relevant to the solution of issues under discussion, and which is clearly presented.

Chapter 18 - Influencing Commercial Negotiations

There are two main characteristics of commercial negotiations which, although not unique to this type of bargaining, have a major influence on its general characteristics:

• Most transactions are concerned with buying and selling, whether of goods or services, or with associated matters such as specifications or delivery. In most cases, the primary factor under negotiation is financial. In most cases, too, the outcome of the negotiation is a legally enforceable contract.
• In many cases, the sole or main reason for a relationship between the two (or more) parties to negotiation is the subject under negotiation.

This contrasts with managerial and industrial relations bargaining, in which the two parties have a working relationship which extends in scope and time, well beyond the narrow limits of anyone negotiating episode.
These two characteristics give commercial negotiations a sharper focus than some other forms of bargaining. During negotiations, either party has the option of abandoning the situation and seeking a buyer or seller elsewhere - an option not open in managerial or trade union bargaining. There is a simplicity in the final deal – in essence, a Yes to a price. To this is coupled a need for precision about the parties' mutual commitments (about quality and delivery, for instance) because these are contractual obligations which, if needs be, must stand the test of the courts.

There is a further point: that the balance of power in a buying/selling relationship is often in favour of the buyer, whereas in managerial and industrial relations situations, the distribution of power is usually much more difficult to assess. Of course, the advantage is sometimes with the seller when a buyer's requirements can be met from only one source. Generally, though, the seller starts with the built-in disadvantage of having to overcome the buyer's resistance, while knowing that the buyer can turn to alternative sources of supply. Training in the skills of selling has, consequently, attracted far more attention than the art of buying. There is an extensive literature on salesmanship, but on buying, the bibliography is all but non-existent.

Sales techniques

This book is not intended as a manual on sales negotiations, but a summary of the selling ploys suggested by much of the literature and sales training programmes illustrates the effort needed to overcome the seller's normal disadvantages:
• Avoid or reduce the direct effect of competition with other suppliers by projecting your product or service as unique. Emphasize the differences between your product and its competitors - not the similarities.
• Flatter the buyer as a person of wisdom and discretion who is able to perceive the advantages your product has over its competitors.
• Stress how your product will improve the buyers' position in relation to their competitors, or will reduce their costs or improve their image.
• Make the buyers feel uneasy about not keeping up to date with new products and developments. Suggest that their competitors may steal a march on them by getting in first.

• Suggest that delay in placing an order may have the disadvantage of an impending price rise or delayed delivery - or that an immediate order will carry unusually favourable terms.

Put as simply as this, these may seem like the crude, doorstep practices of the double-glazing sales person. Yet in essence, ploys of this kind lie behind much of the bargaining of the apparently more sophisticated world of large-scale commercial negotiations.

General bargaining principles

A broader set of principles can also be distilled from the commercial literature, and a number of these points have an application beyond the world of business negotiation.

• Do not negotiate if you can obtain your objectives some other way. Why get into a situation in which you may have to make concessions, or agree to compromise, if you have the ability to obtain what you want without bargaining?
• Do not enter into negotiations without very thorough research and planning. Be prepared - have all the necessary facts and figures at your disposal, and be clear about your objectives and upper and lower limits.
• Try to create a pleasant but business-like climate: do not be provoked into unpleasantness or aggression.
• Maintain the initiative. State your important major requirement firmly and at an early point, thus forcing the other party to take on the harder task of trying to obtain concessions.
• Reveal the strength of your position by degrees: seek agreement primarily by the logic of your case, rather than by threatening sanctions. Use raw power sparingly.

• Look for ways of giving the other party some sense of satisfaction or achievement - perhaps on aspects of only minor importance to you - so that they are conditioned to make complementary moves towards your position. Trade concession for concession.

• Leave yourself room for manoeuvre, either by asking for more than you would ultimately be prepared to accept, or by including some peripheral elements in your claim which you are prepared to abandon if, in so doing, the main objective can be achieved.

• Retain your integrity. Although negotiation may involve tough talking and manoeuvre, never use false data to support an argument, and if you make a commitment or promise, keep it. Effective bargains are all but impossible to conclude if the two parties do not trust each other's statements or intentions.

• Try to listen more than talk. Ask questions more than make statements. The more you listen, the more you will learn about the other side's case, and the less they will learn about yours.

• A void an impasse by having alternative ideas or topics to switch to if confrontation or breakdown seems imminent.

• Allow time for the other party to come to terms with your stated objectives. Do not press too hard for agreement while they are adjusting to the nature or size of your opening bid.

• Clinch agreement at a favourable moment when the bargaining relationship is on a high: and do so briskly and positively, closing the door on renewed discussion.

Contractual implications

It has already been noted that most commercial negotiations result in an agreement which is contractually enforceable. The agreement itself may be in the form of a legal contract document, such as results from the negotiation of a building lease between landlord and tenant. But agreements can be backed by the force of contract law when there are no formal contract documents - only, say, an exchange of letters - or even when no documentation exists. A verbal agreement by an office manager to a verbal offer by a contractor to clean the office windows for a quoted sum, can be enforced through the courts if either party claims the other is in breach - provided they can convince the court of the existence and terms of the agreement.

This emphasizes, of course, the value of putting agreements in writing at the earliest possible date, and of the written agreement being very specific and avoiding ambiguous or vague wording. Where goods and services are concerned, the detail is often best set out in a detailed specification. The agreement, which may be by a formal exchange of correspondence, can then state that such and such a service or product will be provided 'in accordance with the attached and agreed specification'.

In the absence of clear documentation, questions sometimes arise as to whether or not a contract has been concluded. If the terms of a contract are unclear, a dispute may arise about its meaning. These problems are avoidable, but not all managers understand the essential features of contract law. While the complexities which can arise through litigation occupy many legal volumes, the basic principles of contract are very simple - and very important. They are:

• A contract is concluded by a process of offer by one party and acceptance by the other. The agreement must involve 'consideration' - normally, some form of payment.

• Unless specifically stated to the contrary, the contract is concluded at the time of acceptance, whether or not this is documented. If this immediate and binding obligation is to be avoided, then words such as 'subject to contract', or 'subject to written confirmation' must be used.
• If either party fails to fulfil their side of the bargain, the other can pursue the matter in the civil courts.
• Two legal remedies are open - an injunction which orders the other party to perform their side of the bargain, or to desist from action which prevents the bargain being met: or compensation for losses sustained by the failure to perform.
• A dispute about the interpretation of the terms of the contract can also be taken to the courts for resolution. The courts adopt a commonsense approach to such disputes. They ask either, what did the parties intend; or if even this is not clear, what would a reasonable person conclude that the parties intended.
• Contracts will be held to be invalid at law if they include unlawful or illegal provisions, or if one party has led the other to conclude an agreement by deceitful or dishonest means.

All this supports the advice by experienced and effective commercial negotiators that agreements should be in writing, specific in their terms, avoid ambiguity, and be concluded on the basis of an honest presentation of relevant information.

Key points

• Commercial negotiations often differ from other forms of bargaining in that the two parties have no working relationship outside the issues under negotiation.
• The most common feature of commercial negotiations is buying and selling - often to produce a contractually binding agreement.

• In buying and selling, the balance of power frequently lies with the buyer who can choose to deal with an alternative source of supply.

• Consequently, business literature and training programmes concentrate far more on developing selling skills than on the expertise involved in buying.

• Sales techniques include the avoidance of direct competition by emphasizing the unique qualities of the goods or services being sold, an emphasis on the benefits of a deal to the buyer, and encouraging the buyer to make an immediate decision.

• General bargaining principles include an emphasis on careful planning, the trading of concessions and the avoidance of impasse.

• Because most commercial agreements constitute legally enforceable contracts, it is important that they should be in writing, unambiguous, and founded on a basis of accurate information.

• Legal remedies for breach of contract include injunctions to enforce performance, and compensation for financial damages.

• Contracts are legally invalid if they include unlawful or illegal provisions, or were obtained by dishonesty or deceit.

Chapter 19 - Influencing Negotiations with Trade Unions

Negotiations in an industrial relations context can vary from the informal discussion between an individual manager and a shop steward, to a major, national pay-bargaining session between the representatives of an employers' association and a confederation of trade unions. Despite these major differences of scale and style, there are several common features which influence the effectiveness of negotiations. These are:

• The quality of personal relationships between the two parties.
• The existence of agreed negotiation and disputes procedures.
• The importance of precedents.
• The impact of trade union legislation.

Personal relationships

Managers (and shop stewards) who have an interest in the speedy resolution of actual or potential disputes, need to recognize the importance of establishing and cultivating a constructive working relationship with those with whom they may, from time to time, have to negotiate. Personal animosity or distrust creates a barrier to the effective, joint discussion of difficult issues and the evolution of jointly satisfactory compromise. The converse is also true: that if the participants in negotiation understand and respect each other as individuals, the negotiation is far more likely to succeed.

Skilled personnel managers are well aware of this, and work hard to establish a relationship with their opposite numbers on the trade union side which is akin to that of fellow professionals. The underlying attitude is: 'We may be on opposite sides of the table, but we both know the score so far as industrial relations are concerned, and we share an interest in conducting our affairs on a fair, business-like and intelligent basis.' Breakdowns in negotiation can reflect badly on the professional competence of the negotiators on either side.

An example illustrates this cultivation of trust and confidence:

Judith Cliffe was the personnel manager of a company manufacturing components for the motor trade. George Winnall was the factory convenor of shop stewards. The company began to suffer from stock losses from the finished goods stores - probably through employee pilfering. Before taking any formal or overt action, Judith took George aside in the canteen one day and said: 'I don't know whether you've heard anything about this, George, but we may have to come to you formally soon to talk about action to stop stock losses. The security people suspect pilferage, and we may have to consider random searches. You might find it useful to do a bit of scouting around before the next weekly meeting with the stewards.'
A few weeks later (after the stock problem had been resolved without the need for any drastic tightening of security), George called in to Judith's office on an informal visit – she maintained an open door policy for such approaches. After a few minutes of apparently general chat, George said: 'By the way, Fred the Red is up for election as tool room steward next month. He stands a pretty good chance if the tool room manager persists in his daft plan to publicize individual quality records.' George then went on to talk briefly about another topic and then left. At no time had he asked for anything specific.

For the personnel manager in this example to talk about the stock losses in advance of any formally determined action, carried some risks. The convenor might have reacted strongly to the inference that some of his members were pilfering the stock, or even have done something to prejudice the company's investigations of the thefts. But the personnel manager and convenor trusted each other, and this informal contact reaffirmed the trust. Both also recognized, though this did not have to be articulated, that confidences from one party on one topic needed eventually to be reciprocated by the other on some other matter. In other words, what was being created was almost a trading relationship. This was evidenced by the convenor's later hint about the way the election of a confrontational shop steward might be avoided.

Procedures

Apart from very informal negotiations, the processing of most industrial relations issues is governed by formally agreed procedures.
This is partly a matter of long-standing convention, and partly a feature of industrial relations which is promoted by ACAS (in the UK: and its equivalent agencies from the USA, Canada, Ireland, South Africa, Australia, New Zealand and Northern Ireland) codes of practice. The main reason for having agreed procedures is to enable matters to be dealt with quickly, without the need for preliminary discussions about how and when the negotiations are to be arranged. One disadvantage is that a departure from the procedure, however minor, may become the cause of a subsidiary dispute - sticking to procedure having become an end in itself. There are five main elements in most procedure agreements:

• Levels of negotiation: which issues can be negotiated at which levels in the organization's hierarchy. In a large company or local authority, for example, there are often three levels: - workplace, e.g. depot, office unit, workshop divisional or departmental - company or council.

• Participants: who, on each side, takes part in negotiations at each level. For example: - at workplace level, the shop stewards with their immediate local managers. at divisional level, divisional union representatives with divisional managers and their personnel specialists. at company level, full-time union officials, the stewards' convenor, company directors and the group personnel manager.

• Time-scales: a definition of the time periods within which meetings must be arranged after an issue has first been notified by one party to another: and the time limits governing the progression of unresolved issues from one level to the next.

• The conduct of meetings: particularly who will chair the negotiations. This may always be left to management, or may alternate between management and the trade unions, or may (in a few cases, mainly at national level) involve the joint appointment of an independent person such as an academic or lawyer.

• Agenda and minutes: how items are to be submitted for negotiation - whether or not a documented case is needed: the form minutes are to take (brief notes on what has been agreed, and action points; or a full record of the discussion) and whether minutes are subject to agreement between joint secretaries or are left to management to produce.

In addition to the influence of formal procedure agreements in defining the structure and conduct of negotiations, collective bargaining is also influenced by the unwritten ritual of claim, offer, counter claim, revised offer and so on. There is an expectation that a union will eventually agree a lower figure (eg for pay award) than they originally claimed; and a similar expectation that the employer will improve on the first offer. In that both parties are fully aware of these likely moves, they seem to cancel each other out. The routine of high claim, low offer seems necessary -less as a good method of reaching an agreed outcome - than as a ritual which provides a degree of predictability in an otherwise uncertain situation. In recent years, this convention has been put under severe strain by employer or union refusing to move from their opening position. The resentment of the other party to such obduracy has sometimes appeared to be as much a reaction to a failure to play by the normal rules, as it has to the substance of the issue under negotiation.

Precedents

Custom, practice and precedent have a much greater influence on trade union negotiations than in the managerial or commercial fields. Previous agreements, or established practices, tend to be treated as binding (in honour, not at law) until they are superseded by new agreements. This has the advantage of ensuring a degree of stability in the relationships between the two parties. However, it can also create major difficulties if one party comes to consider an agreement or working practice to have become outdated, while the other party (often the trade union) takes the view that the agreement is satisfactory and is, therefore, unwilling to renegotiate the issue.

One way of avoiding such an impasse is for formal agreements to have a designated termination or review date - a practice common in the USA but less used in the UK.

On a less formal basis, both managers and trade union officials tend to refer back to previous decisions, documented or not, as creating rights which can be used as a bargaining factor.

Thus in a construction company, a dispute arose when an employee was dismissed for taking scrap materials from the joinery works. The union's argument was based on established custom, not on the morality of what had occurred.

Employees have been taking scrap for years, said the union official, and the management have turned a blind eye to the practice. The management attempted to counter this by producing records of two resignations of employees which, they said, had occurred only because the employees had been caught taking scrap and had resigned to 'jump the gun' on what would otherwise have been a dismissal.

In the resultant negotiations, as much time was spent arguing about what had happened in the past as on the particular facts of the case which caused the dispute.

The common trade union position is that if something has been done in a particular way in the past, then any change must be subject to negotiation. The management position is often that if evidence can
 be produced to show that the change is not wholly without precedent, then no negotiation is necessary. Arguments about these conflicting views are singularly unconstructive, particularly if they result in a secondary dispute about the existence of precedent, rather than solving the matter in hand. The effective manager will understand the influence of precedent, will recognize when the trade union has the power to block or limit management action, and in those circumstances will enter negotiations with a plea to concentrate on the issue under dispute and the future, not on post-mortems of previous decisions.

Trade union legislation

Legislation has had a growing influence on the conduct of industrial disputes. The law has not impacted directly on the conduct of negotiations, nor has it made collective agreements legally binding. These agreements still lie outside the purview of the law of contract which is so powerful a factor in commercial agreements.

What the trade union legislation has done is markedly to reduce the power of trade unions to take coercive action against employers, and to strengthen the ability of employers to use the law against such action. In short, the legislation has altered the balance of power in favour of employers. Two weapons have been made available to employers:

• *Injunctions:* these are orders of the court to desist from, or to take, specified action. They are very powerful instruments since to ignore them amounts to contempt of court for which the courts have unlimited power to impose penalties - including imprisonment.

• *Damages:* these are orders to pay designated sums in compensation for financial losses.

In outline, the particular features of trade union legislation are:

• It is not unfair to dismiss employees who are on strike, providing all are treated equally.
• Trade unions can be injuncted, or sued for damages, for taking industrial action if this action adversely affects an employer who is not directly involved (i.e. secondary action).
• Trade unions can also be injuncted or sued if they initiate industrial action without first conducting a ballot among the employees concerned. The law prescribes in considerable detail how such ballots are to be conducted, and unions can thus be sued for failing to meet these conditions.

This book is not the place for the lengthy legal exposition which would be needed to set out all the implications of this legislation. The subject is referred to here as a reminder to negotiators that legal rights and duties are a factor meriting close consideration when planning a negotiating strategy. Expert legal advice is essential before launching court action, but on a more informal basis, management negotiators may sometimes need to let the union negotiators see that they are aware of the limitations the law now imposes on industrial action. For example, a threat of immediate strike action might be countered by a comment that: 'You do know that it is now unlawful to start a strike without first holding a ballot?'

Whether such a comment would improve or exacerbate the negotiating climate is, of course, a matter for judgement - but there are still some lay union officials who do not fully understand the extent to which coercive action has been circumscribed.

Key points

• The effectiveness of negotiations with trade unions is affected by the general quality of working relationships between managers and trade union officials.
• Effective management negotiators cultivate a positive relationship of mutual trust and respect with their trade union opposite numbers.
• The processes of formal negotiations are normally the subject of agreed procedures.
• These procedures determine the various levels of negotiation within the organization's hierarchy, who the participants are, time-scales, the conduct of meetings, and the form of documentation.

• Industrial relations are strongly influenced by custom, practice and precedent. General disputes about precedents can become as significant as the issues surrounding specific cases.

• Trade union legislation has severely limited the ability of trade unions to take coercive action, and has, therefore, altered the balance of power in favour of employers.

• This legislation may need to be taken into account when evolving negotiating strategies, and some union officials may need to be reminded of its existence.

Chapter 20 - Negotiating Skills

As in most human activities, some people are inherently better at negotiating than others, but to describe the personality characteristics of the effective negotiator is of little assistance to those whose personalities differ. Personalities cannot be changed. However, that is not to say that negotiating skills cannot be acquired or improved. With preparation and training, most managers can improve their skills in this important aspect of managerial activity.

There are three broad factors involved, each with several elements:
• *Knowledge:* of negotiating principles of the context of the particular negotiation of the detailed subject matter involved
• *Skill:* in analysing the issues in personal interactions in communicating
• *Attitudes:* towards the negotiating process towards the specifics of each negotiation towards one's own role.

Knowledge

No manager can feel confident and at ease in a negotiation without a broad understanding of the general context in which the negotiation occurs. As earlier chapters of this book have pointed out the managerial, commercial and industrial relations worlds all have their particular characteristics and conventions. A manager who does not understand the contractual implications of commercial bargaining, or who fails to appreciate the importance given by trade unions to the existence of precedents, runs the risk of major errors in bargaining tactics, however good he or she is as a 'natural' negotiator.

There are three areas of knowledge to consider:

• Negotiating principles which are characteristic of the particular context. In industrial relations, for example, it needs to be recognized that a trade union derives power and authority from its members - not from its paid national officials. Power in trade unions is derived from the bottom up - the opposite of the company system in which power flows from the top down. Failing to understand this can result in great frustration for the manager who expects the union general secretary to exercise executive authority - when in fact, this apparently powerful union leader has to refer negotiating concessions back to a committee or even by ballot to the whole membership.

Similar misunderstandings can occur between managers who fail to appreciate the conventions of decision-making within the firm, or commercial negotiators who do not understand the technical, legal, or organizational constraints involved in the type of transaction concerned.

• The context of the particular negotiation. Effective negotiators understand the culture, conventions, constraints and opportunities surrounding each negotiating episode. They also ensure that they are fully briefed about every surrounding feature which may impact on the particular issues under discussion. Who are the personalities on the other side? What are their negotiating strengths and weaknesses?

What issues apart from those under direct discussion are of interest or concern and which might influence the way the bargaining proceeds? What sequence of events triggered the situation which led to the need to negotiate? Will the stance any of the negotiators takes be influenced by considerations of status, friendship, rivalry, animosity or ambition?

• The detailed subject matter of the negotiation itself. The effective negotiator has a mastery of the subject under discussion, knowing that an ability to display an in-depth knowledge of the issues contributes powerfully to bargaining credibility. To go into negotiations without this depth and accuracy of information is extremely risky, and will probably be exploited by a skilled opponent.

A managing director met a trade union delegation, without preparation, to discuss their claim for two extra days' holiday at Christmas. 'If it was a matter just for this firm: he said, 'I would be sympathetic; but as you know, we have always kept to national agreements and I can't depart from that now.' The trade union leader responded: 'You seem to be overlooking an addendum to last year's national agreement which made it clear that the annual leave provisions are distinct from any supplementary leave companies may grant at Bank holidays: so you haven't a problem, and we'll accept your offer of two extra days at Christmas!'

Part of the planning process for a negotiation is, therefore, to list all the information which is relevant and ensure that this is obtained (and is accurate and up-to-date) before negotiation begins.

Skill

While certain aspects of negotiating ability may come more naturally to some people than others, skill can be acquired or improved by training and practice. Three types of skill are particularly important:

• *Analytical skills.* Some negotiations may involve consideration of a very complex interaction of various aims and concessions. An effective negotiating plan will, therefore, need to look analytically at the situation and consider questions such as:

- What is the central issue? What are the peripheral issues?
- What is the central objective? What are the subsidiary aims and to what extent can these be traded in for the main objective?
- What are the main barriers to achieving what we want?
- What are the outside limits of an acceptable agreement?
- What are the best tactics to achieve our main aim? How can we make most effective use of sanctions and concessions?
- What alternative approaches are there? What are their strengths and weaknesses?
- Where are we most vulnerable? How can we best protect ourselves?
- What information do we need to support our case? And to undermine the other party's position?
- What are the arguments and information most likely to be used by the other party?
- What contingency plans are needed should we fail to reach an acceptable agreement?

• *Interactive skills.* This is the main area in which some people have natural talent but in which all can improve with positive effort, practice and training. Good negotiators develop an ability to sense and influence the changing moods and concerns of individuals and groups, and encourage progress towards consensus. Much of this skill stems from particular ways of behaving, and although training in these skills is very much a matter of practice and coaching – rather than just reading about them - there are some behavioural traits which are worth remembering!

- A negative habit is to over-personalize issues, by an inappropriate or too frequent use of the words 'I' and 'You'. Thus a manager may say: 'I cannot afford to go beyond 6 per cent', or 'It's not my policy to offer discounts for prompt payment'.

This habit can be intensely irritating when the other party knows that the limits being described derive from team, or corporate decisions or policy, and not from the personal authority of the speaker. Similarly, to respond to a proposal by the other party with 'I do not understand how you can justify that claim', is unnecessarily personal and provocative.

A more impersonal and tactful response would be: 'That is a new point which needs more explanation.'

The effective negotiator concentrates on the *issues,* not on the personalities.

- The temptation to score debating points can be very strong - and is usually best resisted. It can be very satisfying to spot a flaw in the other side's logic and to point this out in a somewhat gloating fashion. It is often better, though, to raise the point by asking a question which will allow the other party to correct their mistake without loss of face. Thus: 'We don't quite follow the logic of that point. Could you explain in a bit more detail?' - rather than 'Do you realize that you have just contradicted yourself!'

- It is also tempting to spend time trying to allocate fault or blame. So a negotiation about new safety measures may become bogged down in arguments about who was to blame for a recent accident. Generally, the better course in this type of situation is to say: 'Don't let's spend too much time on the past. We agree that improvements are needed. Let's concentrate on what - A very important skill to develop is that of listening and questioning, rather than interrupting other speakers with counter arguments, or making lengthy statements. There is no great mystique about acquiring this skill - it is very much a matter of being aware of its value and exercising self discipline.

- A skill in which training is more likely to be required is the recognition of 'signals' - verbal or non-verbal- which indicate changes of thought or mood among the participants. There is a considerable literature on body language, and many clues as to how a negotiation is progressing can be picked up by observing changes in posture and gesture.

Allied to these skills of observation are those of use. For example, a point can be given emphasis by tapping one's papers; and attention can be gained and held by leaning forward and making direct eye contact with the other party.

- It is conducive to constructive discussion to end statements or comments on a positive, rather than negative, note. Thus, instead of saying: 'We are ready to consider your revised proposals about delivery schedules, but the bulk discount is still unacceptable', reverse the statement and say: 'The bulk discount is still a problem, but we are ready to consider your revised delivery proposals'. A negative end to a statement is likely to generate a negative response - and the reverse is also true.

• *Communicating skills.* The ability to communicate effectively is part of the wider range of interactive skills just outlined. But negotiation involves written communication and documentation as well as face-to-face discussion, and clarity of exposition merits emphasis.

There are two common failings: the use of unnecessarily formal or stilted language, and a tendency to be too indirect in relaying bad news.

A shop stewards' committee will not be impressed by a statement saying that: 'The company will have difficulty meeting your aspirations for this year's pay award due to the past six months of negative growth in sales volumes and operating margins.' Better to tailor the language to the audience, and not wrap up an unpleasant message in jargon, by saying: 'We cannot afford the pay increase you have asked for because sales and profits have fallen.'

Attitudes

All behaviour is influenced by attitudes. However skilful a negotiator may be, the application of this skill will be affected by the person's underlying attitude to the negotiating process, the particular features of the matter under discussion, or their own role and motivation.

• Some managers have an underlying resentment about the need, in some circumstances, to negotiate. It is an attitude which has a particular impact in the field of industrial relations. A manager's perception of the role of the employer may be basically authoritarian - that employees should have an undivided loyalty to their employer, and be ready to do what managers tell them. If this attitude is strongly felt, it will be difficult for the manager to accept that employees collectively (through their trade union) can challenge management's ability to manage and have a right - or have acquired the power - to negotiate. Any managerial concession will be thought of as weakness, rather than as constructive compromise.

• There may also be specific features of the negotiation in hand which influence how the participants behave. A manager will become defensive about a feature of which he or she feels a sense of ownership - for example, a procedure or piece of equipment which the manager designed or selected. Changes may then be resisted, not on the merits of the argument, but on the basis of personal pride. Strong personal animosities (or friendships) between individual participants will also influence how they interact.

• Managers may have their own personal needs for recognition or achievement - a perception of themselves as good debaters, or wheeler-dealers, or persons of importance. A negotiation can become an arena for the demonstration or realization of these roles, rather than as a collaborative process to achieve an outcome which satisfies both parties. It is significant that when Lord Goodman (an outstandingly successful legal negotiator) was asked what the most
important aspect of negotiation was, he replied with an attitudinal point - 'the determination to reach agreement'.

Key points

• Although some people are better natural negotiators than others, negotiating skills can be acquired or improved by practice, coaching and training.
• There are three main elements involved in improving one's negotiating abilities - knowledge, skills and attitudes.
• Effective negotiation demands a knowledge of the principles of the negotiating process, the context of the particular negotiation, and its detailed subject matter.
• The main types of skill involved are analytical, interactive and communicative.
• Negotiations are strongly influenced by underlying attitudes to the process itself, to the issues and personalities involved in the particular case, and by one's own self-perception and personal needs for recognition and achievement.

www.ingramcontent.com/pod-product-compliance
Lightning Source LLC
Chambersburg PA
CBHW051507170526
45166CB00001B/432